Tails From Sparky's Doghouse

STORIES OF A MAN, SOME HAM AND A GREAT LITTLE BAR

John W. Carlson

ISBN: 150056916X
ISBN 13: 9781500569167
Library of Congress Control Number: 2014913984
CreateSpace Independent Publishing Platform
North Charleston, South Carolina

This book is dedicated to Nancy B. Carlson, my wonderful wife, frequent dinner partner at the Doghouse and personal editor, without whom this little book would include many extraneous words.

It is also dedicated to all the hungry and thirsty people who were ever on their way to a fast-food joint for a Coke and a Big Mac or a Whopper, and then thought, "What the heck, let's just go to Sparky's for a Bloody Mary and a ham sandwich instead."

FOREWORD

By former Indiana Gov. Mitch Daniels

I'll never forget my first glimpse of Sparky's. As a no-name, first-time political candidate, I was roaming the state in a Hoosier-built recreational vehicle we called RV One, and we often stopped impromptu at places that looked interesting. All it took for me was a look at the name, and I told my road buddy Ben that we had to drop in.

We never went near Mount Summit again without at least poking our heads in. Later, as governor, my one hobby was riding my motorcycles, and it was fun to take my Saturday morning bike crew to Sparky's for the famous bluegill. It was on one of those trips that I got my friend's sweet wife Susie to sample some Rocky Mountain oysters. When she found out what she was eating, she was temporarily upset, and has never let me forget it.

Over a decade on the road, I got to know almost every little diner and dive in the state of Indiana, and I can testify that Sparky's ranks with my very top favorites.

INTRODUCTION

This is a book about Sparky's Doghouse and the man who owns it, a man who, as you may have already surmised, is named, or at least nick-named, Sparky.

Sparky, we should note up front, is a Hoosier, meaning he is from Indiana. But more to the point, it also means that he is a person who dearly loves basketball and breaded tenderloin sandwiches, though he may love ham sandwiches even more, and is what some folks would call "down home," too, meaning he is a friendly, funny, unpretentious individual.

By the same token, the Doghouse is a Hoosier place, more specifi-cally a classic small-town Hoosier place, meaning you could describe it much the same way you do Sparky, it being a friendly, funny, unpreten-tious saloon.

Anyway, though he would probably be too embarrassed to acknowl-edge it, a lot of people love Sparky, just as a lot of people love his Doghouse. What's more, the man and the place are kind of a matched set, it being hard to imagine one existing without the other.

Picturing Sparky as an accountant, a plumber or a preacher, rather than a barkeeper ... well, it just doesn't compute. Neither does picturing the Doghouse as, say, a service station or a place to get a pedicure.

In this book, then, I am going to write about them both, because I, too, am a fan of them both. I am also going to write about some other like-minded folks – most of them living, some long gone – who I have encountered or learned about in putting this story together.

As for why I feel it is important to do so, I sometimes worry that such places as Sparky's Doghouse won't always be with us, which will be a shame. Granted, mine may be the fear of a 63-year-old Luddite who finds the digital social-media age and much of what comes with it scary, depressing or at least fairly incomprehensible.

But what the heck ...

Anyway, you can keep your Facebook, tweets and Twitter. These days, I think there is much to be said for a place where a friend is on the next stool, and Sparky is just across the bar.

John W. Carlson

HOW TO GET THERE

Sparky's Doghouse is located in Mt. Summit, Indiana, about five miles north of New Castle, the Henry County seat, on Ind. 3.

But heading from Muncie, where I work as a feature writer for a newspaper called The Star Press, you go the opposite direction, Mt. Summit being about 10 miles due south.

A four-lane highway with a few gentle turns, Ind. 3 starts out relatively flat, but soon enough begins to transect gently rolling hills, presumably where the Ice Age glaciers failed to level things out a long, long time ago. As you motor along, farms pass by, working operations with corn and bean fields, plus feed lots and pastures inhabited by grazing cattle colored mottled black and creamy white. There are also other farm animals that occasionally are picked off by the coyotes that seem fairly widespread in these parts, making them less than popular with the farmers.

The dwellings, farmhouses or not, run the gamut from modern and prosperous looking to historic and just plain timeworn, but it is always an interesting drive, and frequently a beautiful one. Come spring and summer it's joyously green, a place smelling of growth and cooled by westerly winds that riffle through the thick woods standing wherever you look. In the fall, it's flat-out gorgeous as those woods ignite with broad swaths of reds, yellows and oranges, a natural painting where the finer details are daubed by the autumn wildflowers that border the highway or clump in the fields.

Also in autumn, the drive takes you past at least one orchard where the trees are heavy with honey crisp apples which – as their name implies – are so sweet and crisp, you want to eat them by the bagful. They also provide an ecological life lesson, since it wasn't long ago that a drought totally wiped out the crop, a taste tragedy that, for anyone addicted to apple pie, took a large bite out of the season's joy.

While it's there year round, come late fall you are also reminded that just beyond the woods to the east, there's a Christmas tree farm where the conifers, from shin-high to over your head, grow in endless rows that families navigate to cut down their own tree as the holiday nears.

And then there is winter. Come winter, the snow storms blast in from the north and those refreshing winds of summer can howl and bite like banshees. Then, frankly, the drive sucks.

Anyway, following Ind. 3 south for 10 miles leads you to an exit where, if you turn left, it takes you to Summit Lake State Park and a nice little place to fish.

To get to Sparky's Doghouse, though, you take a right and are immediately in Mt. Summit. It's a small town, to be sure, with only a single caution light flashing yellow on the main drag, but with many of the requisite highlights of a tiny burg in rural Indiana. There's a lot selling used farm implements, for example, one with a preponderance of old tractors that most likely have seen the end of their plowing days. There's a Marathon gas station, too, and a general store that includes your ubiquitous Hoosier Pizza King, plus a big red-brick building with stout white columns called the Prairie Township Community Center, a splendid-looking edifice that, while maybe short of opulent, looks fine enough to seem almost out of place here.

On the western edge of town, meanwhile, is Mt. Summit's largest structure, the abandoned tomato processing plant. A beige-colored, slab-sided facility of multiple appendages that used to pump out seas of Brooks ketchup, it's a place that now serves only as a silent reminder of better days, economically, for Small Town, America.

But wait!

If you've reached this point, you've gone past Sparky's, so turn your car around. In seconds you'll come back to a squat white masonry structure on the south side of the street, one that likely has a pickup truck and motorcycle or two parked along its eastern side, and maybe more directly across the street in a dirt and gravel parking lot. This, you will suddenly understand, is Sparky's Doghouse, because "Sparky's" is painted on the building in bright red script, followed by "Doghouse" in blue, with "beer-liquor-wine" added for good measure.

The rest is easy. Park your vehicle and get out. Then just open the door to Sparky's if it's not already open, walk inside and take a deep, appreciative breath, for you have just entered what is also known as The Cultural Center of the Universe.

THE CULTURAL CENTER OF THE UNIVERSE

It may be sort of hard to understand how Sparky's Doghouse got its moniker, The Cultural Center of the Universe. Chances are if you walk in and try to engage its patrons in a discussion of Elizabethan poetry, Wagnerian opera or even the best – or worst - of modern-day cinema, you are going to be answered with a blank stare, a turned back or even a request that you please go bother somebody else.

Still, The Cultural Center of the Universe is what it's come to be considered by those in the know.

This also has nothing to do with the décor, by the way, which can be summed up as Early 21st Century Dive Bar.

Yet, the place's fans, and there are a whole bunch of them, wouldn't have things any other way.

Walking in the eastern entrance, you pass the battleship gray partitions that shield one's view of the men's and women's restrooms, step past a well-used Brunswick heavy slate pool table and, in a few steps, are at the Formica-topped bar, along which perhaps 10 barstools are aligned. To their backs, the room's heavily scuffed checkerboard floor is filled with four or five tables, one of which, in a corner, is the official site of the morning card players, older gentlemen, mostly, who pass the hours over hands of euchre and cups of strong coffee, their wives undoubtedly having urged them out of the house.

Sparky calls them "The Mooreland Euchre Academy," in recognition of and homage to a nearby town.

Near where they play is the Doghouse's Information Center, housed in a wooden cabinet that Sparky, who is a fine woodworker, built himself. The well-perused tomes resting within it include the "Indiana Basketball Encyclopedia," "You and the Law," "North American Wildlife," the "Reference Guide to Firearms Parts," the "Blue Book of Gun Values" and "The Baseball Encyclopedia."

"At one point we had a Bible in there," Sparky said, "and it got *used*."

There is also a solitary carving of a solitary clenched hand, save for a solitary middle finger, which is extended straight up, an apparent reminder that, regardless of what you might think of yourself, you're probably not all that special.

While the Doghouse has a library of sorts, then, what it doesn't have is a juke box, which is kind of a sore subject with Sparky.

"That's right," he said, when a visitor observed this lack of what normally is regarded as standard tavern equipment, sourly alluding to the musical tastes of some of his younger patrons. "And we're never *gonna* have one, either."

Rather, whatever music you hear here is provided by the bar's single small television set, which can be tuned and locked into a country music or golden oldies channel.

"That way, we get to listen to what we want to at the volume we want it," Sparky continued, noting he once did have a juke box here – for all of two weeks. "It caused a lot of my customers to get up and leave. I told them to come take it away. It did nothing but cause trouble."

Heading from The Mooreland Euchre Academy's table back toward the bar, you pass the front door, which opens to the north, and then a large cooler filled with cold beers, the most exotic of which is Stroh's, unless you count the hard ciders. There are also assorted sodas. Then you make your way behind the bar past a couple condiment stands bearing ketchup and mustard bottles and salt and pepper shakers, as well as a slotted plastic box holding a handful of change and couple dollar bills donated to a Bible-buying society. Keep stepping in the direction of the ancient black grill, then, which has seen incalculable use over the years, until finally you are about to enter Sparky's tiny office, where he works on the books.

The space against the wall behind the bar is worth describing too, though, so let's back up.

The cash register is there, of course, along with a state lottery machine and other necessities of the barkeeper's trade. Small packages of aspirin. A spice rack. Another rack, one with a plastic covering that is open at the bottom and holds cigarettes, all of them Marlboros of assorted strength, flavor and packaging. Near it are Bic lighters, kid-proof ones with safety latches that make them pretty much adult-proof, too, latches that bartender Steve Houser will kindly disable for fumble-fingered smokers, using a stout pocketknife he carries.

There's liquor, too, of course, on shelves bearing assorted sized bottles of Jack Daniels corn whisky, Jim Beam, Wild Turkey and Old Grand-Dad bourbon, Southern Comfort, Bacardi rum and Dark Eyes vodka, among others. Plenty more are stored underneath it in closed cabinets that Sparky made himself. A word to the wise, though: If it's a mixed drink you want, keep it simple, like a rum and Coke.

Ask for a Perfect Rob Roy on the rocks with a twist, and all you are going to get for your trouble is a funny look from your bartender..

High above the bar, meanwhile, is a trophy shelf of sorts with a couple fancy – or maybe corny is a better word - decanters, such as an Old Crow one that looks like the specified bird dressed as a dandy. There is also a mounted record-setting bluegill the size of an NFL-regulation football and some wooden signs, going back years, bearing the names of customers who have won the Doghouse's popular Tea Pot Open Golf Tournament.

"And if you're a very good golfer," Sparky warned, "you can't play in it."

Alongside them sits the famed trophy itself, a pewter tea pot, dull silver except for the dark holes where it was peppered by buckshot.

Somebody found it out in the woods.

Also up there is the electric sign that announces Doghouse news flashes in a continuing trailer of colorful points of light, including everything from who won what in the monthly drawing to the bar's personal check-cashing policy. It also reads, "Come to the Doghouse. You're only a stranger if you wear a tie."

Meanwhile, hanging behind the bar with the attractive calendar model who forgot to wear any clothes to her photo shoot, are your requisite bar signs.

"Free beer tomorrow" is one.

"How do I spell relief? F-A-R-T" and "This is a work-free smoke-place" are two others.

"Complaint department CLOSED" reads a third, decorated with an intimidating image of Yosemite Sam.

"Hot beer, lousy food, bad service," reads yet another. "Have a nice day."

And, of course, there's one reading, "Don't worry if you're lost, someone will tell you where to go."

But the funniest is the wooden sign hanging under that small television set up high in the corner.

"If idiots grew on trees," it reads, "this place would be an orchard."

SPARKY

"If I ever win the lottery, 85 percent of it I'll spend on whores and whiskey and gambling," Sparky has been known to say. "The rest I'll blow on things I *don't* need."

He delivers that line with a sort of deadpan dryness that catches you off guard, cracks you up and, if you happen to be writing a book about him and his saloon, sends you scrambling to get it written down.

Robert Lane Harris can be a very funny man.

Walk into the Doghouse and you can't miss him behind the bar, and not just because he's the only guy there wearing dark red suspenders with "Sparky's Doghouse" embroidered on them in electric lime green. Handsome in a way that's almost reminiscent of the late great Errol Flynn, with a face that tends to redness and hair and a mustache that are going to gray, he stands a solid, towering 6-feet-7. Having been born on May 28 in 1950, he has been around for 64 years, 99.99999 percent of which he has been known as Sparky. His father, Robert E. Harris, was a railroad man and a coon hunter who was famous for his ability to tell a good story, a trait he surely passed on to his son. He was also a man adamantly opposed to having a Junior in the family, but was an equally avid fan back then of some little musical spark plug who played the piano on the radio from a station in Cincinnati, a kid named Sparky.

"My father just started calling me Sparky," said Sparky. "It lacks about three days being as old as I am."

Consequently, say "Sparky" around these parts, and pretty well everyone knows who you are talking about, just by that one name.

"I always said it was like Ralph Liberace," he explained.

As he spoke he was seated at a table in his tavern, a place he hasn't owned all his life, but definitely has for most of it.

Raised in the Henry County town of Cadiz, where his family lived in the telephone exchange, a place of old fashioned plugs and wires that his mother, Ruth, worked like the ones you see in classic movies, he went to school there and in Sulphur Springs before heading to Shenandoah High School for his senior year.

Like most Hoosier boys across the state, from early on he played basketball. Unlike most Hoosier boys across the state, he got good at it, eventually competing for Edison Junior College in Florida before returning to Indiana, where he played for Butler University in Indianapolis his junior year. Though he left the university his senior year, he still has a soft spot for the place, as is evidenced by the two basketballs displayed in plastic cases above the Doghouse's Information Center. Both are signed by the Bulldog teams that made it to the NCAA championship games.

"I wouldn't take anything for them," he said of those basketballs, having obtained them with the help of Bruce Horan, a friendly young man who also played for Butler in far more recent years and who, having bought The Ice House bar in New Castle, considers himself something of a Sparky protégé.

When Sparky came home, however, it wasn't with hoops on his mind. He needed to earn a living.

In 1973 he hired on at Rural Electric Membership Corporation, better known as REMC, going to work as an electrical lineman. But he also had his eye on a saloon called the Doghouse, where he had tended bar part-time as a 21-year-old. Back then, he said, it had a reputation as having once been "a blind tiger," or bootleg joint. It had also been well known to Sparky's contemporaries.

"Every kid in the county lived for the day he could come in and drink a beer here," he recalled.

About this same time, Sparky was also working with an older friend, a farmer named Royce Alspaugh, with whom he would buy feeder pigs and raise them for market.

The Doghouse, as it turned out, kept weighing on Sparky's mind, until there came a Saturday at the farm when he mentioned the tavern to his friend.

"You know," Sparky told him, "we ought to buy that place."

Alspaugh's reaction was, "Well, I'll put the money up if you'll run it."

Now, in the years since then, Sparky has developed a reputation as a shrewd businessman, one who can be careful with a buck when the need arises. But it was a more impetuous Sparky of that day, just a kid, really, who went to see the bar's owner, Mentis Huff.

"So like a fool I offered him too much money," he recalled, noting that amount was $70,000, which was actually $10,000 more than Huff wanted for it. "It took him 90 seconds to say yes."

And just like that, on Dec. 16, 1974, at all of 24 years old, Robert Lane Harris launched his career as a small-town saloonkeeper.

The day Alspaugh's loan was approved Sparky quit the electric company without regrets, climbing utility poles having gotten old fast. The farmer had mortgaged 50 acres of land to get the loan.

"He pitched me the keys and said 'Don't screw it up.'" Sparky recalled.

The very first morning he opened, he got a hint of what lay in store for him when an employee of a nearby sawmill came in, eventually having a surplus of drinks lined up on the bar before him. The guy finally poured them all into one of his dirt-covered and undoubtedly odorous boots, raised the boot to his lips and chugged them down.

Later, naturally, he passed out on the commode so nobody else could use it.

For some folks, it might have seemed an inauspicious start to a brand new career, but not to Sparky. At that point, he figured, with fellows like that guy around, his business was bound to thrive, and pocketed the man's $1 tip.

"I kept that first dollar for a long, long time," he said.

N*u*TS

Joyce Dishman is known as Joy, but equally well known around Sparky's Doghouse as "Nuts."

"I always say she got her nickname the old-fashioned way," Sparky jokes. "She earned it."

If you paid attention to the cars out front as you parked, you knew she was inside, since the Indiana license plate on a certain white Cadillac reads I R NUTS, which should answer any questions about whether she takes offense at her nickname. This Monday at lunchtime she was one of three people sitting at the bar, eating a deep-fried breaded tenderloin with a knife and fork, hold the bun. It was an unusual day for her to be here, since she normally only comes in on the first Saturday of the month, helping out when the place attracts a boisterous crowd for a drawing that can include winnings of up to $300, as well as meat – steaks, chops, bacon, you name it – supplied by her brother, Bob Dishman, who owns a nearby meat locker.

The infrequency of her visits notwithstanding, she knows Sparky pretty well, having been his significant other for 15 years now, though their association goes back considerably longer than that.

"I've pretty much known him all my life," she said, reflectively, lighting a thin cigarette and explaining that she grew up as one of 10 children in a family that took its religion very seriously. Then she smiled. "Sparky was always that bad man who had the beer joint."

Now?

"The whole family loves him," she said, this despite the fact most of them remain non-imbibing religious conservatives.

After so many years together, Sparky remains clearly smitten with her, in a way that he figures paying a visit to a preacher couldn't improve.

"I always tell folks that the only thing married people can do that we can't is get divorced," he said.

Joy has two sons from a previous marriage, one living in Indianapolis and one living in Germany, now-grown men Sparky refers to as Lugnut 1 and Lugnut 2. Sparky is close to them, and regularly visits the one in Germany with Joy. Her two grandchildren live in Germany, as well, and Sparky adores them, considering them his grandchildren, too, taking particular delight in their effortless verbal exchanges of English for German and vice versa.

Talk to Sparky about those kids and his eyes light up with warmth and pride, as you would expect of a man who is just a nice guy to be around. It's sort of amazing, then, when Joy talks about others' reactions when they began going together.

"Some of my girlfriends, when they first met him, they were *scared*," she recalled. "Now they think he's nothing but a big teddy bear. He's just the most generous person that you could ever know. He'll help anybody at any time."

Tales of his generosity abound, including taking care of the insurance for Timmy Howe, a former bartender now wheelchair-bound from the effects of a stroke. Sparky also bought him an iPad with a voice rehabilitation app that helped him regain a level of understandable speech. Then there is Sparky's relationship to Dee Dowling, his trusted second-in-command, for whom he has promised to keep the Doghouse going until she reaches retirement age.

"She's my ace in the hole," Sparky said. "She's my trump card."

Joy's take on her? "She runs the place when Sparky is gone. She pretty much runs it when he's here, too, if you want the truth."

Sparky is also even-tempered, something of which Joy, an attractive, slightly built woman with a quick laugh and warm eyes that easily flash with humor, seems to particularly appreciate.

"He never raises his voice to me," she said. "He doesn't get mad."

This is even more impressive when you know that Joy, a soft-spoken woman whose friends all say is as sweet a person as has ever walked the proverbial earth, has absolutely nailed Sparky with impressive, elaborate practical jokes at least a couple times.

By now, these are the stuff of Doghouse legend.

One involved a gasoline nozzle and length of hose she obtained, then stuck in the fuel access port of Sparky's car after what had been a night of revelry at the Eagles Club. Next morning, a guilty-looking Sparky woke her in a bit of a panic, asking if he had gone back out the night before.

Indeed, she answered, he had.

"Hon'," he continued, before sheepishly leading her out to show her the wayward nozzle, "I want you to come out here and see what I've done."

It was an embarrassed Sparky who finally headed back to the gas station, circled slowly around the pump that had been marked "out-of-service," then finally schlepped inside to confess his role in its demise to the station's owner, Mike MacAlister, a longtime friend who had secretly provided the length of hose and nozzle to Joy.

When MacAlister started laughing, it became clear to Sparky that he'd been "had" by Nuts.

"I can't believe you would stoop to that bitch's level," Sparky told his buddy, but to Joy he said only, "OK, the joke's up."

But at least that prank was just among a few friends. What you might call "The Case of the Diehard Skunk" was played out on a bigger stage.

One day Joy, who does all the yard work around their house, discovered that a skunk had been living under their tool shed. Telling Sparky about the critter, he secured a trap to dispose of it, although Joy soon learned that a neighbor had already removed it.

Failing to inform her own true love of this important fact, however, she opted instead to buy some black and while fabric, forming it into the shape of a skunk with a wire hanger, then stuffing some red fabric inside it and even rigging it to a remote control device that, when activated, made it shake.

Then she invited a bunch of folks over for an outdoor breakfast.

Sure enough, they were all collected around the back yard that morning when Sparky discovered the trap had been sprung.

"Punkin'!" he hollered in victory, using his other pet name for her. "We got the skunk!"

With the breakfast guests, all of whom had been clued in, chuckling and watching, Sparky the Skunk Terminator noted the beast was shaking with rage in its cage, casually announcing to the crowd that yes, when it came to trapped skunks, that was their common reaction. Then he grabbed his rifle.

BLAM! Still the intrepid skunk stood.

BLAM! Some red stuff came out this time, but still the skunk was standing.

BLAM! And what should suddenly come flying out of the skunk's innards but ... batteries?

The crowd, of course, cracked up. Sparky's only comment to Joy, who had spent 15 years working at Ball State University in housing, dining services and on the grounds crew before quitting, was, "You need a job, woman. You've got way too much time on your hands."

Right after that, he opened a Curves gym for women in New Castle for her to run.

"He bought me a job," Joy said with a smile.

HAM

Walk into Sparky's Doghouse about any hour of any day, grab a stool at the bar, then take a gander at the opposite counter to the immediate right of the grill, and you're going to see a substantial hunk of baked meat.

It's a ham, one of Sparky's famous ones.

But that's not to say it's the only meat you'll find here. Look up and to your right and there is a menu posted on the wall, one full of the bar food you might find in many Hoosier taverns. There's a hamburger and cheeseburger, of course, and a substantial ground steak sandwich, a grilled pork tenderloin sandwich, plus the requisite breaded pork tenderloin sandwich, which is pretty much Indiana's official state food. The Doghouse, I am told, has a darned good one, with Sparky pounding out and breading each one by hand.

There's also a sausage sandwich that has plenty of fans and lots to commend it. A length of kielbasa, or maybe Polish sausage, if there's a difference, it is butterflied and its skin scored with a knife to keep it from curling up when cooked, which is accomplished by dropping it into the deep-fryer. There's an extent to which the guys who buy this crispy brown beauty are considered culinary daredevils, it seemingly possessing the ability to clog one's arteries almost instantaneously.

The real culinary daredevils, though, are the folks who take this a step or two further, combining their deep-fried sausage with, say, a breaded pork tenderloin plus some other pork product, all on the same bun, creating mouthwatering mountains of porky mayhem known variously as the Porkinator or Pork-a-saurus.

You won't find either of those on the menu, by the way. You have to ask. Anyway, add an order of deep-fried cheese sticks and maybe a Bloody Mary or two, and you've got yourself the makings of a meal that, if nothing else, will kill you with a smile on your face, and all for a very reasonable price.

What's more, though, you can often eat at the Doghouse without spending a dime. Saturday mornings, Sparky cooks up a substantial breakfast of eggs, fried potatoes, bacon and even sausage gravy and biscuits, allowing his patrons to help themselves for the bargain-basement price of nothing. Nada. Zilch.

They just have to pay for their coffee.

This isn't the end of his largesse, either. Sometimes he'll make huge pots of chili, or a potato soup for which he is locally famous, or even huge tubs of a favorite pasta-garden salad, and pass those out as well. Meanwhile, an old buddy of his named Dan Peyton has been known to bring in bluegill that Sparky fries up and serves for nothing, little filets that his customers who have sampled them can't talk about without salivating.

Other times he'll be down at the end of the bar, grinding away with a food processor, then come bearing a loaf of fresh wheat bread and a huge pan of ham salad, a tasty home recipe containing eggs, pickles, cheese and horseradish in which the prime meat is actually bologna, with maybe a small slice of ham tossed in.

"A very small slice of ham," Sparky emphasized, "for ceremonial purposes only."

But, of course, we can't forget the "mountain oysters," also known, of course, as testicles. Back in the day, when farmers used to raise hogs for longer lengths of time before castrating them, they would deliver some healthy-sized balls to the Doghouse for frying.

"I've had five-gallon buckets of nuts before," Sparky said, discussing how they would clean and prepare them for cooking.

But now that hogs are being castrated at younger ages, when their testicles are less developed, he's more likely to get calf nuts, which are meatier, larger-sized spheres of yummy goodness.

Either way, as most folks who have tried them will attest, balls can be darned good eating on a sandwich, even if they don't necessarily taste like chicken.

"We've never had anybody I know of get sick from eating testicles," Sparky added, which is a ringing endorsement if we've ever heard one.

But back to ham ...

Forgive the biblical-sounding reference, but in the beginning, Sparky bolstered his menu with a big ground steak sandwich that proved to be a winner.

"They went like wildfire," he recalled.

But along about the mid-1970s, he had another idea, this involving a similarly big ham sandwich.

"I had seen 'em do it in Indy at Shapiro's," he recalled of that world-class delicatessen, located just half-a-mile or so south of Monument Circle, where the corned beef and pastrami sandwiches are legendary. "I thought, if it worked for them, it had to work for me. I had worked at Marhoefer (Packing Company) and I knew how to bone a ham."

What he wanted was a ham sandwich that would sate the hunger of the big old farm boys who worked up hellacious appetites out there in the fields. Sparky began buying Emge hams, 17- to 21-pound ones, and baking them with a top-secret beer recipe, one he won't reveal, sort of, to this day.

"We always tell 'em it's an ancient Chinese recipe, which is three cans of beer in the bottom of a pan. It might be two Stroh's and a Budweiser, or it might be two PBRs and a Stroh's," he teased, before admitting to at least one trade secret. "But that goddamn Heineken don't work."

He bakes these hams for about three-and-a-half hours, and has been doing so to the tune of more than 100 a year, just for the sandwiches sold at the Doghouse.

It is, indeed, an impressive hunk of meat that greets you as you walk in, a dark pink ham in a crisply baked skin nestled in a shiny metal holder that, depending on how many ham sandwiches he has served that day, may be nearly full or trimmed down to where its bone protrudes from the top like a handle, which is convenient for carving.

Order a ham sandwich and Sparky or whoever is making it will attack that upright ham from the side, using a knife to cut off thin slices to fry in a stack on the grill. Equally important as thin, however, is maintaining a nice even, level slice, sloping ham being something that offends Sparky's natural sense of culinary propriety. The most level cutter on the Doghouse staff earns the mythical Herman Reese Award, which Sparky named after a fastidious butcher in Sulphur Springs.

"As far as I know," Sparky said, "I'm the only guy in the world who cuts their ham this way."

At any rate, from the very start the ham sandwiches went over even better than the steak sandwiches did. Now, they are something of an institution hereabouts. There is almost always a ham available, and often a new ham cooking, thanks to their reputation. In fact, Sparky can walk into many taverns within a 25-mile radius and somebody will say, "There's the ham guy."

Even the bread deliveryman eats a ham sandwich at the Doghouse every day, which Sparky considers irrefutable proof of their quality, since that fellow is in and out of eateries all day long. Then there is the Canadian couple who, having been lost near the Doghouse years ago, stopped in for directions and tried the ham sandwiches. Now they pass through twice a year like clockwork, once on their way to vacation in Florida and once on their way back home to Ontario. Each way, they stop in for beers and a couple more ham sandwiches, which comes as no surprise to Sparky.

"That's our signature sandwich," he says.

Only rarely does he find himself faced with a hungry customer and that day's ham still baking in the oven, but it has happened.

"We have people who, if it ain't done, they won't eat," he said.

Things only got busier years ago when a member of the Doghouse family died and Sparky, not wanting to send flowers, sent the mourners a fresh-baked ham instead. Now he dabbles – or more than dabbles, actually - in the ham catering business. Whenever a friend or good customer dies, a free ham shows up for their family, one that Sparky has expertly sliced and artfully arranged on a tray. Its reputation is such that, when a former big-time Hoosier politician's wife died a few years back, the family requested one of Sparky's hams.

These days Sparky can dress a ham in 15 minutes, which for the math challenged, is a rate of four an hour. That's a good thing since, once word of his funeral hams got around, folks began ordering them for the holidays, too. Come Christmas he'll cook 50 or more of them at $65 each, hams he lovingly arranges on trays under protective plastic covers and stores in the beer cooler until folks come to pick them up. Buy one and he also throws in a nice bag of the ham scraps, for inclusion in beans and such.

"They paid for the ham," Sparky said. "They get the scraps, too."

At any rate, just in case we failed to mention it, Sparky's ham sandwich is a memorable, great tasting one, a sandwich that the man himself, or Dee Dowling, or Robin Wilkerson or Karen Drumm behind the bar, will expertly put together, slide in front of you on a classy piece of waxed paper and leave, knowing you are going to love it.

Bill Kinnitt certainly did.

A former bartender here whose son, Gary Kinnitt, had worked the bar, too, Bill had eaten a lot of Sparky's ham sandwiches in his time.

"He loved 'em," Sparky recalled.

After his retirement, Kinnitt became one of the corner card players but was eventually diagnosed with cancer, waging the good fight until, finally, his doctors told him there was nothing more they could do, and that he should go home and put his affairs in order. He was being taken to his Sulphur Springs dwelling in an ambulance when he demanded a detour, telling the driver to instead head to the Doghouse.

He wanted one last ham sandwich.

The ambulance guys did just that for Kinnitt, who died a few hours later.

"They said he could only eat half of it," Sparky remembered, with uncharacteristic quiet. "I'm sure it was quite possibly the last bite of food he ever took."

HIZZONER

It's amazing the people Sparky's Doghouse brings together. A lot of them are farmers and other working-class folks, as Sparky proudly notes. They are men and women with hard-won skills, people whose hands are trained and capable of producing the vital things of life, things that some might be inclined to forget in this day and age when we have experienced a sea change, transitioning from an America that used to make things to an America driven by a service economy.

"I'd say on any given day here at lunch you could get a house built," Sparky will tell you, and he's not kidding. "Virtually any blue-collar job is represented here. Carpenter. Plumber. Electrician. Painter."

On the other hand, those workers also mix easily here with regulars who may include executives, teachers, physicians, bankers and such folks as you might more likely expect to find at the country club, and sometimes do.

But even so, it's not every country saloon in Indiana that can boast of a former governor who is a fan.

Sparky's Doghouse can.

That all started back when former Gov. Mitch Daniels, a Republican, walked in one day before his first election, campaigning for votes. Truth be told, he probably knew he was playing to his people, conservative small-town and country dwellers with a bedrock belief in traditional values.

"President Obama takes an awful beating in here," Sparky has been known to say, though not unkindly.

Anyway, Daniels schmoozed the crowd and even managed to impress some folks with his appetite for bar food.

"That little bitty guy, he ate four or five sandwiches," Sparky recalled of that first visit. "He likes the place."

What's more, there were subsequent visits, some when Daniels was campaigning, others when he wasn't.

Gary Demaree remembers one particularly well.

Now an investment manager in Muncie, a while back Demaree had worked in radio and later in public relations for Ball Corp. An Indianapolis resident for a short period of time, Demaree noted his father, Jack, had been involved there in a men's group at a United Methodist Church with one Richard Lugar, who soon became that city's mayor. Later, when the Demarees returned to Muncie, Jack and Lugar stayed in touch. Eventually, Lugar decided to run for the U.S. Senate.

"The only guy he knew over in our area was Dad, who jumped right in," said Demaree, who occasionally helped out his father, in the course of which he met Lugar's campaign manager, a bright young guy named Mitch Daniels.

The rest, as they say, is history.

"I've known Mitch for many, many years," Demaree said.

Anyway, the two renewed acquaintances a few years back when Daniels spoke at a Rotary Club function in Muncie, and since both are Harley-Davidson motorcycle enthusiasts, the talk finally got around to, "You get out to ride much?"

When that led to the possibility of meeting up on the road somewhere, Demaree recommended one of his favorite spots, Sparky's Doghouse.

At this, Daniels' eyes lit up. "I've been there!" he said.

Within a month, Demaree received a call from a governor's aide to set up a rendezvous. Demaree called Sparky with the plans, then on the appointed day led a bunch of friends who were riders, including educator Dick Daniel and a local judge, to Sparky's. Arriving, they found two stern-faced, plainclothes state troopers sitting where the guys of The Mooreland Euchre Academy normally sat, and looking not all that happy to be there.

Soon, however, Daniels pulled up out front on his customized Harley, one on which the state seal of Indiana had been embroidered into the seat, and accompanied by some friends who were fellow bikers.

What was it like?

"We just had a nice time," Demaree said, noting the governor fit in perfectly, talking and joking with the regulars who were there. "It was no formal thing. He didn't want it to be a public affair. He was in a black T-shirt, jeans and a ball cap."

Sparky, it should be noted, pulled out all the culinary stops, in the Doghouse's own way, for his special guests. There were all the normal menu items, of course. But then he cooked up a mess of Dan Peyton's melt-in-your-mouth bluegill, too, then topped it all off with the *crème* d' la *crème* of tavern cooking – a mess of nuts, as in testicles.

These days, of course, Daniels has vacated the governor's office for the presidency of Purdue University, but he left behind some special keepsakes of his visits, and memories as well.

In a book Daniels published about his first election campaign and ramblings across Indiana, there's a photo of him with Sparky.

There's also a rather historic picture of Daniels and another legendary Doghouse character, Whitey Shively. While he was an auctioneer by trade, his daughter found success in Hollywood, where she had been hired as the casting director for one of Indiana's favorite movies, "Hoosiers." It, of course, is based on the story of little Milan High School's 1954 upset state-championship victory over a basketball powerhouse, the Central High School Bearcats of Muncie.

In that movie, it should be noted, the Bearcats aren't called the Bearcats, and Milan is named the fictional town of Hickory.

Anyway, thanks to his daughter, Shively played the Hickory team's doctor who temporarily took over after star Gene Hackman's coach character got bounced by the refs. "To Whitey, an Indiana Legend," Daniels wrote on his photograph.

To Sparky, meanwhile, he sent a post card, one the saloonkeeper treasures to this day.

"Sparky," it reads. "We all enjoyed last Saturday's visit. Good times, great eats (especially the appetizers). You might get some first time walk in customers someday soon because I have been talking the place and bluegill up everywhere I go. Off to China this weekend, where I won't be eating nearly as well. Cheers, Mitch D."

Sparky will be glad to show you the postcard, if you care to read it.

"He's a pretty nice guy," he said, proudly, of our former governor.

KEEP PEDALING, DUDE

For Gary Demaree to get to Sparky's Doghouse in the first place, he had to find it. Luckily, John Coers had given him directions years earlier.

For the record, a sizable contingent of Muncie folks makes its way down to the Doghouse on a regular basis for food, a beer or two and to recharge their batteries amongst Sparky, Nuts and any other regulars who happen to be on hand. While many of these folks drive cars and trucks there, a number also make their way riding cycles, as we noted with Demaree and our former governor.

In that, Coers, who works as a laboratory scientist for Indiana University Health Ball Memorial Hospital, sort of led the way, except he did it on a bicycle, not a motorcycle.

This all started when he and some neighbor buddies began riding bikes for exercise and decided, to make it more palatable, to include visits to country bars on their otherwise healthy excursions. One of those riders, Tim Kelley, had a father named Ham with an encyclopedic knowledge of such classic places, and he recommended the Doghouse.

"He used to work for a freight company," Kelley said of his dad. "He knew all the pubs in all the towns around here. He'd have lunch, entertain customers."

The word on Sparky's Doghouse?

"He said Sparky was a character," Kelley recalled.

So that is why Coers and company made it one of their very first stops, it amounting to a nice 30-mile round trip from their homes.

Well, all you have to do is picture that group of middle-aged men entering the Doghouse, sweating, heaving, wheezing and walking stiff in their hip- and butt-hugging Spandex riding shorts, to imagine how Sparky, whom Coers had never met, extended them a warm and sympathetic Doghouse welcome on their first visit, inquiring as to how he could possibly help them.

Just kidding, of course.

Indeed, from the start, as Coers recalled, Sparky was on them like white on rice, mercilessly making fun of everything about them, undoubtedly including those Spandex hot pants.

"That's old Sparky," Coers reflected recently. "He's crazy."

Of course, there's also something about this place that, despite the ribbing, in just one visit set them well on their way to becoming regulars. One likely reason? The comforting consistency of the Doghouse.

"I think he bought some new barstools once," Coers said of Sparky. "Other than that, I don't think the footprint of that place has changed at all."

Then there's the food. While Kelley is not a regular anymore, he still recalls the free casseroles Sparky would dish up, not to mention the fresh fish.

"It was amazing," he said.

The mellowness of the place is another reason, as was demonstrated one day when Coers was dumbfounded to hear Kelley blurt out, "Sparky, how do you get enough hillbillies to play in that golf tournament of yours?"

This comment was greeted with pregnant silence by the burly country folk eating lunch around them, but in the end, nobody smacked anybody upside the head with a pool cue.

The best reason they adopted it, though, is probably just Sparky himself.

"You know how he is," Coers said. "He'd pretty much give you the shirt off his back if he could."

Oh, and one last reason. The Doghouse is the place to go if you want to walk in the steps of greatness, or at least in the steps of 1960s heyday-of-professional-wrestling greatness, a time preceding Sparky's ownership. Coers said that back then, he was told legendary wrestlers like Dick the Bruiser, The Crusher and even Bobo Brazil, would meet up at the Doghouse after matches in New Castle to grab a beer and a sandwich and divide their earnings.

Bobo Brazil? In the Doghouse?

Wow.

By the way, Coers couldn't recall if The Sheik had ever showed up, too, but how cool would that have been?

EIGHT BALL

Thursday nights at Sparky's feature the sharp clicks of pool balls colliding, that sound signaling the Doghouse's weekly tournament night. "It's always eight-ball, single elimination," said Steve Houser, a friendly guy with combed back salt-and-pepper hair who this night was filling in behind the bar.

His opinion of this place?

"It's just a friendly down-home bar," he said, serving a visitor the hamburger he had just fried him. "Everybody's like family here. We don't have anybody that starts any trouble. No bullshit, I guess."

He seemed to have the operation of the Doghouse well in hand. Usually, though, the Thursday night bartender is Karen Drumm.

Here at the Doghouse, where nicknames seem to abound, hers is simple, yet unforgettable: Cheeseburger.

What's more, it wasn't bestowed on her by Sparky. She's had it since she was 10. "A lot of people don't even know my real name," she said with a laugh. "I guess I don't look like a Karen after being Cheeseburger for so long."

If Sparky didn't nickname her, however, he did nickname her daughter who, being a pint-sized version of her mother back in the day, became known around here as White Castle.

Get it? A smaller cheeseburger?

At any rate, it was Karen who started the pool tournament a few years ago.

"I kind of took a little survey for about a week," she said, adding what she found was that people wanted a tournament. Unlike the cutthroat nature of some others, however, this one emphasizes fun, drawing as few as four and as many as 18 players on any given Thursday.

Getting in costs $6.

"It's not like the leagues," she said. "It's just something fun to do on Thursday nights. It's very laid back. Nobody from Sparky's is ever going to make it to Vegas, but we have fun."

While Karen started it, she is usually too busy behind the bar to actually run it, which is where Melissa Klein steps in. It is she who keeps the brackets, collects the entry fees and such.

"And try to keep the games moving," she added.

Speaking to Melissa over a cell phone, one couldn't help but feel hunger pangs as she noted she was, at that moment, in the process of delivering 80 handmade pizzas that were stacked in her car, all part of a fundraising effort for her daughter's school band.

Her husband, Kevin, is active in the tournament, she noted, as he was back when a friend of theirs who originally kept the books suffered a heart attack.

"I kind of just took over," said Melissa, who away from the Doghouse works in reception, and grew up around Mount Summit, where the tournament can be something akin to a reunion.

Not everybody who plays in it is from there, though. There's even a fellow from Italy – his name is Mario, naturally – who lives in New Castle and competes occasionally, she said.

If Melissa's association with all this began with someone's heart attack, Karen's working association with the Doghouse began about six years ago with another medical crisis, right after she nursed her significant other back to health from cancer.

"I went in there one day to pick up a sandwich and Sparky, who I'd known as long as I can remember, asked me why I wasn't working," she recalled.

With her man having recovered and just returned to work himself, she noted she needed to get back to earning a living, too.

"I went down there for a tenderloin and came back with a job offer," she said, though she admitted at the time she accepted it with some reluctance.

What does she think of her decision now?

"It's the best job I've ever had," said Karen. "Sparky? He's an original, that's for sure, and Nuts (who is a good friend of hers) is just nuts. Now, I just wouldn't change a thing. I wouldn't change a thing."

SHORT TAKES

Barney Black's key to headache relief, as told to Sparky: "Just drink three drops of whiskey in nine ounces of water. If that doesn't work, reverse the process."

Sparky, on his work and how it appears: "To the untrained eye it looks like I'm having a good time. It's called public relations."

Overheard in the Doghouse, according to Sparky: "Do you remember your first piece of ass?"
Old man at the bar, incredulously: "Are you kidding? I don't even remember my *last* piece of ass."

Nicknames of four house painters who are regular Doghouse customers: Rembrandt, Picasso, Remington and Van Gogh.

Byron "Fat" Brown was a memorable customer, Sparky says. Weighing in at about 350 pounds, he could put fully a half-sack of chewing tobacco in his mouth at one time.
"If he didn't have a chew in his mouth," Sparky added, "his jaw just kind of hung there like a pouch."

Sparky, on breaking up fights: "I've been hit in the ribs with a pool cue a time or two, but that was mostly in the early days."

Dealing with aging customers: "Forty years ago I bought a tavern. Now I've got a convalescent center."

Miss Patty, on the stupidest call she ever took at the Doghouse: "What time is the 2 o'clock drawing?"

Sparky, on how alcohol affects speech: "They say there's no word in the English language that rhymes with 'purple.' People who believe that have never been drunk at the Doghouse."

Sparky's take on how booze affects IQs at the Doghouse: "Nine o'clock in the morning, you can't find anybody smart enough to tell you what time it is. By 2 o'clock, they're all geniuses."

Sparky, on nicknames: "His nickname used to be Wiedemann's 'til he quit drinking beer. Then we called him Pepsi."

George Bowers was one of Sparky's favorite people. He recalled how once back in the early 1970s they got on a gravel road, decided to see how far they could get without using a highway, and wound up in Cincinnati. They'd also take to lonely roads in Bowers' Cadillac, which he'd steer with his knees while playing guitar and shooting birds off electric wires with a .22.

"We had all kinds of entertainment back then," Sparky remembered, also remarking on shooting rats at the dump. "By the end of the day you were wore out from having fun."

An excited greeting from Sparky to a sometime regular: "Dish! Who put up your bail money?!?!"

Season's greetings: A Christmas card sent to the Doghouse picturing four grinning, long-haired, heavily-tattooed young guys, all in the Henry County Jail, that reads, "From all of us, to all of you." Explained Sparky, "They were all arrested leaving here."

Closing time on New Year's Eve, which should be a major party, according to Sparky: "Whenever the bartender is tired. Usually about 8:30."

Dick Harvey was a good old farm boy, Sparky said. "He had a tractor that wouldn't run unless it had beer on it."

A master carpenter, among the things Sparky has turned out in his shop is a beautiful altar for a small, nearby church. "How many guys build one of them?" an admirer noted.

"Yeah," Sparky agreed, "that own a tavern yet."

Woman eating lunch at the bar: "Too bad you don't have a dog. I dropped a piece of ham."

Sparky: "Don't worry, one of the drunks'll get it."

Two guys came in, one having lost a bet and one having won, the loser paying for the winner's lunch.

"What's the most expensive thing you've got?" the winner asked.

Sparky pointed to Nuts and said, "She's sitting down there at the end of the bar eating a sandwich."

Gary Demaree: "I like Sparky because he's just a down-to-earth, say-it-like-it-is kind of guy. He is a man of his word and a man of really great character."

One day a fellow rode a horse through the Doghouse, "Just to show everybody how gentle his horse was," Sparky explained.

The result?

"Oh, it caused one hell of a ruckus," Sparky said, recalling one customer's complaint. "You don't let me bring my damned dog in here, but you let him bring in his *horse*?"

Sparky recalled one lovable old bartender – "He was an alcoholic, but he couldn't help it" – who bought his wife a fancy food processor for her birthday, then couldn't remember where in the Doghouse he had hidden it. In time, the man died, and eventually Sparky found it, and the loving birthday note that went with it, stashed way in the back of a storage cabinet.

When he took the card and the food processor to the widow, she cried.

Sparky offered a customer some of the ham salad he had just prepared.

The customer asked, "You make this?" to which Sparky replied, "No, it (freaking) appeared that way."

Under no circumstance does Sparky ever drink in his own tavern.

One of Nut's sons has an incredible way with dogs, Sparky said, noting that when his Doberman pinscher misbehaves, all he has to say is "corner" and the huge guard dog stands with his nose in the corner, sheepishly glancing over his shoulder to see if it's time to come out yet.

"I had a doctor asked me if I drank," Sparky recalled. "I said let me put it this way, when I was 21, I walked into a tavern and I haven't come out yet."

Daneeta Phelps on her friend: "I've known Sparky close to a hundred years now."

Sparky's instructions to Marimaude Steadman Culp, after she accidentally knocked over two drinks in a row. "Talk with your mouth, not with your hands." By the way, it was a long time before he started serving her drinks in glasses again.

Marimaude's father, Horie Steadman, was a regular and a favorite of Sparky's, a slow-talking good old boy who was in love with Cher and Dolly Parton. He told Sparky he once had a nightmare that Dolly was his mother and "she was trying to wean me."

By the way, Steadman also once drove directly into a train that was stopped on tracks near the Doghouse.

"That," he complained to Sparky, "is a hell of a place to park a train."

An outright favorite of Sparky's was Barney Black, a Warner Gear retiree and pony racer who was remarkably jovial and fun-loving.

"He was the most perfect retired man I've ever known," Sparky said, noting how Black would come into the Doghouse every day and tell the most fun stories. "I'd have *given* him his whiskey to make sure he'd come in and talk to me every day. Of course, I wouldn't tell *him* that."

A bit of bar wisdom: "If you don't have many fights," Sparky said with a laugh, "you're not selling enough whiskey."‘

All kidding aside, Sparky's Doghouse is known as a peaceful place where nobody wants trouble.

"It's been several years since I've had a fight in here," Sparky said, adding that if he spots anyone carrying a gun in the Doghouse, they aren't going to be carrying a gun in the Doghouse for long.

One key to keeping the place free of – for lack of a better description – jerks, assholes and other assorted miscreants, is barring people, some of whom Sparky has dragged into the street, from the Doghouse. If people have angered him enough to bar them, how long are they barred?

"Three generations," he said. "You, your kids and your goddamned grandkids."

Sparky: "Everybody dies famous in a small town."

Bruce Horan, on watching the very tall Sparky tee up a golf ball: "He looks like a giraffe drinking water."

Sparky, on learning the bar business: "There ain't but one way to learn, and that's to go in there and ram your head against the wall."

Sparky on COPD, the lung/breathing disorder: "I've got it. It's a horrible thing. The only thing I'd like to convey is, anybody who smokes, try to do their best to quit."

He smoked until he was 50, by the way, and has asthma to boot. Thankfully, his COPD is manageable, and his doctor says it isn't getting any worse, no thanks to the Doghouse, where there is plenty of smoking.

"I'm in a hell of a horrible place," he said, for a COPD victim, and tobacco smoke isn't the only culprit. "The deep fryer puts off fumes, too."

Customer E.W. Conner still holds the record for accidentally knocking over barstools in the Doghouse: Five. Thankfully, no injuries were reported.

Sparky on bulls, or giant hogs, or maybe it was Bigfoot: "Anything that weighs a ton and his nuts drag the ground, leave him alone."

Sparky on his popular family name: "I was 25 years old before I found out my name wasn't 'dammit.'"

Sparky's mother, Ruth, was an inveterate bingo player. In fact, she was resting up before heading out for a game when, at 83 years of age, she took a nap and never woke up. A short while later he was following the ambulance to the hospital with his father in the car beside him when the lost old man said, "God damn. Who am I gonna fight with now?"

Lots of people will tell you what a great guy Sparky is, just as a matter of course, but Robin Wilkerson thinks of an immediate, personal example.

"Well," she said, "he mows my yard for me every week."

That's a real blessing for the Doghouse bartender, who takes ongoing chemotherapy for cancer every 21 days, and also has circulation issues that affect her legs.

With more than an acre of yard, mowing it is no snap, even on a riding mower, but Sparky is ever faithful about keeping it trimmed. Wilkerson, in turn, is just as dedicated to the Doghouse.

"As long as my legs will let me," she said, "I'm going to stay there."

Overheard at the Doghouse: "I could have a good time on an iceberg if I had plenty of whiskey."

Dick Patterson, son of longtime Doghouse diner Bill Patterson, seems to have a special connection to the food here. The night of Dick's 1967 high school graduation, a friend of his father's named Ivan Darby bought him a celebratory steak sandwich.

Of course, he had to eat it out in the parking lot, which is where his grandchildren, who are 8 and 9 years old, have to eat the Doghouse ham sandwiches he buys them now..

"They love the ham sandwiches," he said. "They think it's fun."

Female bartender: "Telephone!"
Sparky: "Coming mother!"

Sparky on Buck, who was the proprietor back when it was Buck's Doghouse: "He said there were only two things that ever caused trouble in a tavern. One was a woman and one was a telephone. He wouldn't allow either one of 'em."

From a famous Doghouse drunk who, against all odds, gave up drinking: "What do I notice about not drinking now? You know, I've lost a lot of knowledge."

36

Sparky, on paying for the free food he often provides customers: "Every once in a while, somebody'll throw a few bucks in the pot."

In Doghouse we trust: "If you heard it here, it's gotta be gospel."

One patron was called "the strapless evening gown," because "he had no visible means of support."

Architect Brian Hollars, whose wife is the lovely, inimitable Kelli Jordan, who is also an architect, was brought into the Doghouse for a sandwich about three decades ago by his then soon-to-be stepfather Gary Lambert. Just 16 at the time, he must have figured he used up his luck by not getting bounced on that occasion, because he hasn't been back very often since.

Slogan: "Sparky's Doghouse, where the first liar does not stand a chance."

While cutting up some of his hand-pounded, hand-breaded tenderloins one Saturday, Sparky trimmed a meaty/fatty piece for a visiting newspaperman, then chopped it up and served the pieces to him.
"Cracklins," he explained. Which, by the way, were great.

Speaking of cracklins, a former janitor at the Doghouse named Junior Darby loved them, but would pour so much pepper on them nobody else could stomach them. Darby was tougher than your normal customer though, Sparky said. His fingers were so callused, he picked them out of the deep fryer without getting burned.

Real down-home cracklins are just the cure for constipation, Sparky added: "They'll make you shit through a screen door at 90 paces and never touch a wire."

Sparky: "An earthquake hit Kentucky one time and did $250 million worth of improvements."

Phyllis Broyles has traveled with Sparky and Joy to Las Vegas and elsewhere, and known him for years. "Sparks a good buddy. He's just like a brother."

Asked for a favorite story about Sparky, Daneeta Phelps paused and said, "There are so many stories about Sparky." She, too, has traveled with Sparky and Joy, and says he is a great tour guide.

"He's traveled enough that he can show you things," she said.

She visits the Doghouse every month for the monthly drawing, and also goes a few days before that, since to keep her same numbers – which have won her the drawing a couple times – she must sign up for them by the Thursday before.

When she does, she usually eats one of his hand-pounded, hand-breaded tenderloins, but adds, "The ham is outstanding, too."

Another good thing?

"He has a knack for getting good bartenders."

Broyles added with a laugh that, "I'll be going until I can't go any longer, or until my play money runs out."

Sparky, on the ailing customers who are always warmly welcomed here: "Yeah, we do a lot of therapy up here. We kind of act like a family unit for a lot of folks."

Sparky, on good-natured ribbing inside the Doghouse: "Nobody who comes here is spared anything. If you've got a flaw, don't ever bitch about it."

Sparky used to make a practice of giving out small gifts – money clips, ashtrays, beer mugs, screwdriver sets – to his customers at Christmas, but no longer, something he blames on the salesman.

"The goddamned guy died on me!" he explained.

The fishing trip note that a friend of Sparky's left for his wife: "Went fishing. See you next week." Turns out, the trip was to Canada.

Sparky, on parental discipline: "My parents won't let me misbehave – Mother Nature and Father Time."

Worthless things, in Sparky's estimation, an issue raised when Gordon H. Carlson of Elyria, Ohio, was in the Doghouse dining on a ham sandwich one Saturday. He noted we were four days away from May 28, the 69th anniversary of the day that he, a 19-year-old Navy gunner at the time, was wounded, plus half his gun crew killed, when a kamikaze struck his ship in the battle for Okinawa: "A milk bucket under a bull and a helmet on a kamikaze pilot are the most worthless things I can imagine."

If you have a memory like an elephant's, you'll recall that May 28 is also Sparky's birthday.

A great description of Sparky's Doghouse: "Mt. Summit's version of 'Cheers.'"

Sparky, on a place he once visited: "There must be a nuclear waste site around there somewhere. You can't find that concentration of idiots without something being wrong."

One block west of Sparky's Doghouse is the reason the town is called Mt. Summit. It's the railroad track, which happens to be the highest rail point in Indiana.

Sparky's opinion of why the Doghouse is like some high-powered think tank: "There's just all kinds of wisdom comes out of this place. There are a lot of great thinkers come in here."

Here's an interesting fact you won't hear about a lot of taverns. Sparky once tabulated the total, and figured 15 to 20 millionaires have patronized the Doghouse, a figure that includes bankers, farmers, the owner of a car dealership and guys connected to the Shively clan, of whom Whitey had a role in the aforementioned film "Hoosiers."

Even more interesting?

"We've had about the same number (of people) we knew, for a fact, had killed another human being.

Bruce Horan, one of Sparky's protégés and the youthful owner of The Ice House in New Castle: "I can't even imagine the Doghouse without him."

Sparky on an inveterate liar: "I can always tell when he's lying. His lips are moving."

Sparky's mother once said he had the greatest accumulation of useless information she had ever known.

Sparky, on a certain woman he really, really, really dislikes: "She's got a disposition like a rattlesnake with an abscessed tooth."

Sparky, on a certain female acquaintance's tush: "Her ass is, like, two ax handles across."

Sparky, on one customer's appetite: "If the son of a bitch don't fight back, he'll eat it."

A young woman recently left the Doghouse only to find she had a flat tire, so naturally the patrons helped her change it. "This is a full-service beer joint," Sparky noted.

There was a street department worker from New Castle who was famous for the way he always observed his payday. "What day is it?" the clientele would holler, just to witness the over-the-top way he would rear back, hold his arms out for emphasis and roar, "*FRIDAY!!!!!!!!*"

So one Friday when he came in, a chorus of customers bellowed, "What day is it?" and he answered, "I don't give a (you know what)."

Turns out, he'd retired.

Jack Pherson, on what keeps bringing him back to Sparky's Doghouse: "We come over here to get verbally abused, and he's good at it."

Bruce Barefoot on what he likes about the Doghouse's cooking facilities: "You see what you get."

Speaking of which, one day Pherson and Barefoot observed a bartender working at the grill drop half a hamburger bun on the floor, then consider picking it up and using it anyway. Turning to them, he sheepishly explained, "The mustard broke the fall," before doing the right thing and grabbing a new bun.

Sparky, indignantly, upon being interrupted: "Wait a minute! Who's telling the lie here? You or me?"

As friends of the Doghouse know, no less a personage than former Gov. Mitch Daniels – who as of this writing is president of Purdue University – has visited multiple times, and even mentioned Sparky in his State Republican Convention speech of 2004.

What drew the governor to the Doghouse? In a book he wrote, he said it was the name.
"Having spent so much time in (his wife) Cheri's doghouse, I couldn't pass it by."

A big, bearded guy, Steve Spradlin and his lovely wife, Allison, have been known to make occasional stops at Sparky's on his Harley-Davidson, a very cool, very nasty-looking motorcycle. Recalling Joy's interest in natural things, Spradlin remembered she once gave him a bird identification book.
"That's where I learned the state bird of Oklahoma is the Scissor-tailed Fly Catcher!" he excitedly announced, a sentence we're quite

sure no other Harley-Davidson owner has ever uttered here - or anywhere else, for that matter.

Derrick Wright, the son of Stuart Wright, who won the meat drawing the first time he ever set foot in Sparky's Doghouse with his Dad, on Sparky: "He's the coolest dude ever."

The incident Stuart Wright most easily recalls from the Doghouse, and one that still leaves him laughing, is the time a guy walked in to a standing-room-only crowd and was effusively greeted by Sparky, who hollered, "Hey, Bill! It's *great* to see you!"

Amazed and humbled by this greeting, the fellow basked in the glow of such recognition, until Sparky then hollered, "Now I'm not the ugliest (a really nasty four-syllable word) in here!"

Sparky joking about the state of his finances: "I'm so poor, I can't even pay attention."

MISS PATTY

Sparky and Nuts have no more loyal fan than Miss Patty.

"To me they're two people that give, give, give with no expectation of anything in return ... and Nuts makes a mean cream of asparagus soup. Sparky's an honest, kind-hearted man. If somebody's in a jam and needs a little help, Sparky will help. I know some that he has helped. He's just got a good heart. He's one of the kindest men I've been around."

Miss Patty, it should be noted, is widely known at the Doghouse, and by that name. What's more, she prefers it that way.

In her workaday life away from Sparky's place, she is what she called a "financial professional," with an impressive title and a very nice office, a comfortable place of earth tones and large picture windows to match her title. Sometimes, she said, she will be in the Doghouse with her boyfriend, Darrell Clark, then run into some fellow stalwart from Muncie's banking community and return their look of surprise.

"Oh my gosh, what are *you* doing here?" they will ask, or she will. "You name it, you just never know who you're going to see here. Lowlifes, highlifes and some that are just medium, but everyone gets treated the same."

In her particular case, she's been coming here since about 1998, when one day she walked in and introduced herself to Sparky.

"Over the years," she said, "it's just evolved into a wonderful friendship."

Indeed, she and Darrell and Sparky and Nuts often travel together on weekends, their closeness attested to by the fact they can be cooped up in a car for four hours straight without feeling the need to constantly talk to each other.

Like Nuts (also called Joy, you'll remember) she has noticed the physical change that slides across Sparky's face like a lowered window shade when they leave town, the tension draining from him.

Perhaps it is because they are so close that Miss Patty is entrusted with a complicated task that's fraught with responsibility - running the Doghouse's regular drawings.

"She's the handiest thing to have around," Sparky said of her. "Trustworthy. She does it right, and just out of kindness. If Patty says something, you kind of want to pay attention to it."

That sort of trust is something she holds dear.

"One Saturday he asked me to help, and I did," she recalled. "Now people call up and ask for 'Miss Patty.' I find it a tremendous compliment that he trusts me. It's unconditional trust."

Sparky's Doghouse holds a Type 2 gaming permit, which doesn't exactly make its owner swoon in undying gratitude to the state of Indiana, which is heavily into legislatively endorsed gambling of its own.

It's not that Sparky sees this as hypocrisy but ... well, yes he does.

"They let us tavern owners have a bologna sandwich while the casinos have a Thanksgiving dinner," is how he puts it.

Nevertheless, the monthly and weekly drawings are held on Saturdays, and often fill the bar with noisy, generally happy hopefuls. Miss Patty moves through the crowd and watches over all this like a protective mother, keeping everything running, taking names and maintaining an orderly flow to the process as folks crowd in, leaning against walls, sitting on the pool table and crowding the corners waiting for the appointed time to arrive.

During this time, people have been known to sit squirming at the bar for hours, steadfastly refusing to use the john since they know their seat will be gone when they get back. At last, Sparky announces the drawing.

"All right, war babies, listen up!" he hollers.

A barstool or two down, somebody says, "He's gonna make somebody in this place happy. God, I hope it's me."

Then with a shake of his jar, he ambles through those gathered for all the excitement and picks the prettiest girl he sees to pull out the winner, whose take is limited by Indiana law to $300.

Sometimes, the winner has a proxy there, meaning their joy is somewhat restrained, as was the case recently when a sweet looking, matronly woman successfully played her good friend's ticket.

"Tell the bitch I won for her," she said, dourly.

That's not all the action, though. As was noted in an earlier tail, um, tale, there are also drawings for significant amounts of meat, everything from ribeye steaks to slabs of bacon, and they tend to stir up a good bit of hooting and hollering, too.

By late afternoon when the action is over and some of the regulars begin to file out, it can be good to step into the open for some fresh air, even if you didn't win anything, there having been a lot of alcohol drunk and a lot of tobacco smoked inside. Sparky may head out, too, looking to spend some time in his woodworking shop or on his tractor.

Still, you leave with a good feeling that pretty much guarantees you'll come back.

Such is the appeal of the Doghouse, whether you win or not.

"It only takes one or two times going in there to feel welcome," Miss Patty said, now sitting behind the desk in her office while assorted employees hustled about their business beyond her open door. "The patrons kind of look after each other, for the most part. It's one of my favorite little places, I can tell you that."

As for running the drawing itself ...

"This is my very favorite thing to do, ever," she said, laughing. "There's no stress, and I still get to interact with people. You can give 'em hell, and they like it."

YOU CAN BANK ON IT

Customers of the Doghouse aren't the only folks Sparky keeps fed. Employees of the Trojan Plaza branch of Citizens State Bank are nourished every Saturday morning, as well.

"He brings breakfast for all the employees at this location," said one of those employees. "He brings food all the time. He's always full of gifts."

This all started years ago out of the goodness of Sparky's heart when one of those bank branches was located in Mt. Summit. Then the branch was closed and its workers transferred back to New Castle, leading one of them to ask him, "Why can't you keep doing that down here?"

Well, that was enough.

"All it took was just a little nudge and he was right on it," the employee said.

That was five years ago, and almost every Saturday since, Sparky has delivered breakfast to the ladies at that branch, for free, of course. If he is going to be on vacation, Sparky has one of his own employees make the delivery, and on the rare occasion when nobody is available to do it, he warns the ladies ahead of time so they can grab their own breakfast that morning.

"He's awesome," said the bank worker, a comment echoed by a co-worker.

"I think it's wonderful," she said of the free breakfast deliveries. "Who *does* that?"

By the way, besides dishes like breakfast sandwiches, home fries, eggs and sausage gravy and biscuits, Sparky will bring corn bread, potato soup, pasta salad and more.

So what does she like most about this?

"I like Sparky's personality, that's my favorite thing," she said, warmly, before being asked why she thinks Sparky does what he does. "I don't know. I think he likes to see us smile. ... And he's a man of habit."

How so?

When he comes in Saturday mornings, she said, the ladies all ask how he's feeling.

His constant answer: "Purdy."

It should also be noted that whenever Sparky returns from a trip to Germany, for example, he always brings the ladies special gifts, like magnetic thermometers that attach to filing cabinets.

"It always makes us feel special," she said.

But, she was asked, magnetic thermometers that attach to filing cabinets? Who has those?

"Apparently the Germans," she answered.

JEN AND STEVE

Jen Stevens and Steve Merritt are a handsome couple, meaning he's all right and she's drop-dead beautiful in a wholesome, all-American way that belies her 47 years. Anyway, they are engaged and, by the time you read this, are probably married.

They are also wonderful, friendly, engaging people. More importantly for the purposes of this book, though, they are fervent fans of Sparky and his Doghouse, which Steve – who on weekdays is a buttoned-down banker in Muncie - used to live near.

For him, a native of Sulphur Springs, Sparky's Doghouse was a fixture of his formative years, not that he could go there as a kid, of course. But once he could, he did.

"It's sort of like an oasis," he said of the place, noting the folks from farmers to doctors who patronize it. "It's a catch-all for a lot of different people."

While most of those folks have undoubtedly heard of the Doghouse's reputation as The Cultural Center of the Universe, he enjoys being there when a newcomer arrives expecting something, well, perhaps more palatial.

"I enjoy watching them look around and say, 'Really?'" he recalled. "'Cause it looks so, um ...'"

We'll just leave it at, um.

But he noted, for example, how a deer head once rested on the bar for a couple of days, almost like a passed out regular. And yes, if you are wondering, it was mounted, not freshly detached.

Jen's take on the place?

"I think it's Americana at its best," she said. "People are only strangers there once or twice. Good people go there. They're just good people."

As a leader of the Doghouse's Muncie contingent, it's not uncommon for Steve, who started patronizing the place when a cold beer would cost you just 65 cents, to step inside and find a dozen fellow Munsonians there.

"I can go in there any given time and I know a lot of people," he said. "It's amazing how many people this place touches."

The folks he knows include employees like Karen Drumm, who he went to school with, and who he steadfastly refuses to call by her nickname, Cheeseburger.

"I just can't do it," Steve said, adding the same holds true for Nuts, or rather, Joy.

At any rate, Sparky's Doghouse has played a role in the Muncie couple's romance.

"I wouldn't say we fell in love there," Jen said, "but we sort of did."

Indeed, she added that at one point, Steve asked Karen to, "Please make Jen fall in love with me."

Apparently, whatever the bartender did worked.

There are a host of obvious reasons why a man would want that to happen, but one you can't discount is her extraordinary luck, at least inside the Doghouse. No better example exists than when they were there for the meat drawing and Sparky asked Jen to act as his ticket drawer for the ribeyes, chops and porterhouse steaks that were being offered.

Oh, and the bacon, too.

"I always go for the bacon," she noted.

At any rate, Jen pulled the first ticket and darned if she didn't win some meat. Then she pulled the second ticket and ... darned if she didn't win some more meat. Then Sparky had her pull the third ticket ...

"And it was like, wait. *What*?"

You guessed it, Jen had won again, but given the silence that had suddenly overtaken the suspicious crowd, she and Sparky decided to give that meat to somebody else.

That was a memorable visit to the Doghouse, of course, but Jen and Steve have had others.

Once they were in there with several other couples, laughing and enjoying themselves as folks in laid-back, small-town taverns are wont to do, when two young, well-dressed and rather arrogant women came in for lunch.

Before long, the regulars heard the young women make a couple offhand comments about them, accompanied by sharp stares of disapproval, before one finally said, "Could you keep it down? My friend here has a headache."

Taken aback, to this they responded something to the tune of, "But ... we're in a *bar*," to which one of the uppity women haughtily spat, "You're all just jealous because we have our own teeth!"

At which point, without missing a beat, Steve Houser behind the bar whipped out his own dentures and replied, "I've got my own teeth, too! Who else has theirs?"

A postscript to the story: Though they hadn't requested as much, Houser packed the women's lunch orders to go and invited them to leave.

Houser, by the way, played a key role in another memorable day for Jen at the Doghouse. It happened one afternoon when she had arrived there while Steve was still on a golf course, so he called Houser and – Jen looking as good as Jen always does - asked him to keep an eye on his girlfriend.

"Will do," Houser promised, or words to that effect, then hustled back to an apartment he rented at the time, which is attached to the tail end of Doghouse. Quickly returning to the bar, he then placed a very realistic fake eye on the bar directly in front of Jen.

Keep an eye on her? Obviously, Houser was a man of his word.

Turns out years before he had lost an eye in a roofing accident, and that was one of several prosthetic eyes he owned.

"WE'VE HAD A MAUDE SIGHTING"

When Marimaude Steadman Culp walks into Sparky's Doghouse, it's rarely unannounced.

"We've had a Maude sighting!" Sparky will holler from behind the bar, a greeting to one of his oldest friends as she heads over and takes a stool. Later he explained, "Maude gets top billing wherever she goes. You can hear that laugh from about a half-mile away."

Once she is on that aforementioned stool, she's happy.

"This is the highlight of my month," she said. "The monthly drawing. All the people that move away, when they come back, this is where they come.'"

How far back do she and Sparky go?

"We started first grade together," said Maude, who now lives in Indianapolis. "And I probably knew him before that."

While moves and such eventually separated them, they reunited later at Shenandoah High School, where Sparky was an unmistakable character.

"He was just so much bigger than the rest of us," she recalled.

Truth be told, though, those early years were not without a level of turmoil between the two, due to one potentially serious conflict.

Maude, it seems, was the only kid at school who could out-hit Sparky in baseball.

Told that Sparky had revealed as much in a conversation, she erupted in hearty, unrestrained, joyful laughter.

"He said he always resented me because the other kids picked me for teams before they picked him," she explained, attributing the resentment he supposedly still felt to his outstanding memory. "He's got a memory like nobody I've ever seen. ... I mean, Sparky remembers the birthdays of people we went to school with. I don't know how he does it."

It was about 15 years ago at a class reunion that Maude met Joy, and they have since become dear friends, too. For her money, that makes Joy the perfect woman for what she considers a wonderful man.

"I'll tell you," she said. "For all his gruff exterior, you will not find a more loyal person, a more caring person and a more generous person than Sparky."

He obviously treasures her, too, something he affirmed one night when they were leaving the Eagles Club together and he put his arm around her.

"Maude," Sparky told her, "whoever thought that after all these years, we'd still be friends.".

TEACHER

The guy three stools down was a fellow in the youngish-to-middlin' spectrum of middle age, still bundled against the cold outside, with a manner about him that suggested a level of education above what you might normally encounter at Sparky's Doghouse on a wintry Tuesday evening.

Sure enough, it turned out that Bob was a Ball State University graduate who had been teaching history and psychology in an area high school for 25 years.

He'd been coming into the Doghouse for years, too, usually just for an hour or two, right around suppertime.

"It's one of those places that, as you become an older guy, it's safe," he explained. "I've never seen an argument in here, let alone a fight. It's not the late-night type of joint. Everybody knows your name."

Bob said he especially liked hanging out with the older guys.

Why?

"I'm *becoming* one of the older guys," he answered, saying the Doghouse is a good place to talk about everything from lousy weather to a rough day at work.

"It's also a good place to network," he added, using a word that probably never would have come to his older buddies' minds, let alone lips.

At most, Bob shows up maybe a couple times a week and said he first started coming when he moved to Sulphur Springs back in 1992.

What did he think of Sparky?

"He's a nice guy," he said, recalling a time years ago on a fishing vacation with his young sons when both boys caught three-foot Northern Pikes. Well, it just so happened that back home, Sparky had a three-foot Northern Pike on the wall of the Doghouse, which led Bob to joke about how good it would look hung on a wall in his kids' room.

Sparky told him to get up there and take down that fish for his kids. He wasn't kidding, either.

"It was probably a $300 or $400 mount," Bob noted, adding the fish wound up on a wall at home where his boys could see it, and relive the day they caught theirs.

So, Bob was asked, Sparky would indeed give you the shirt off his back?

"Or the fish off his wall," he said.

THE MOORELAND EUCHRE ACADEMY

It was a frigid morning during a lousy Hoosier winter, but things inside Sparky's Doghouse seemed cozy as Bill Shafer, 64, a former trucker, Larry Howell, 70, who had been a New Castle fireman and fire marshal, Steve Leffingwell, 71, who worked at Delco Remy, and Bruce Wright, 75, who had worked at Warner Gear, sat at the corner table, drinking hot coffee and playing euchre.

None of them, just in case you were wondering, was playing hooky from work.

"We're all retired," Howell said, as golden sunshine that seemed to make a mockery of the plunging temperature seeped inside the place.

Some of these guys were among the regulars here who seldom if ever take a drink in the place, playing cards being what brings them here.

"I used to come here and drink a lot of beer," Leffingwell admitted, "but now I've kind of quit on that."

Their history at the Doghouse went back a minimum of 20 years, though, and far longer than that for most of them, as Leffingwell noted.

"I remember when Sparky bought this place," he said, leading Howell to note that, "We're the old regulars now."

When Sparky thinks about guys like these, it's with a knowledge of what a place like the Doghouse can mean to folks who don't necessarily have a lot of other convenient gathering spots to choose from. After all, The Cultural Center of the Universe, along with being a bar, restaurant, carry-out store, pool hall, shrink's office and, to reiterate, The Cultural Center of the Universe, is also a social center.

"It's a meeting place, is what it is," Sparky said, adding that he feels like he has a "flock" of folks he looks out for, much like a pastor has one.

That notion of a flock and a pastor seems all the more relevant in this instance, euchre being almost a religious practice among many Hoosiers. Indeed, in the matter of The Mooreland Euchre Academy, its roots could be traced back to big biblical concepts like good and evil, loss and redemption, plus life and even death.

Before the Doghouse, you see, the academy's precursor had met in the town of its origin in a service station's dingy grease room, a place where its original members took their game seriously.

You might even say very seriously.

Actually, it wouldn't be a stretch to say very, very seriously.

In fact, in what became an illustration of exactly how seriously Hoosiers can take their euchre, Sparky noted, one of the original players, having unsuccessfully argued some finer point of the game with another, went to his car, fetched a firearm and shot his opponent to death.

"It's a famous story," Sparky said.

Anyway, it was some time after that when Leffingwell – a guy Sparky said would rather play euchre than eat - came to the Doghouse and asked if what became known as The Mooreland Euchre Academy could come there and play.

"I said, 'Yeah, but I'm not putting up with any fighting,'" he recalled.

Killings either, presumably.

And that explains, to this very day, what those guys are doing most mornings in that corner by the Doghouse's Information Center, though Sparky also offers a different sort of explanation for it.

"We're husband-sitting," he said, starting another pot of coffee and reflecting on their appreciative wives relishing their own free time these mornings. "We watch 'em until it's time to go home."

TOMATOES

Just like you could argue that Ball jars made Muncie what it is today, for Mt. Summit you could argue it was tomatoes, millions upon uncounted millions of tomatoes. The thing is, while you'll still find an active Ball jar and Ball family presence up Muncie way, the only tomatoes you'll find in Mt. Summit are growing in folks' gardens.

Back in the day, though, they raised a bounty of them in vast fields hereabouts, tomatoes that were destined for the now-deserted processing plant on Mt. Summit's near west side. There they would be turned into that delicious tomatoey condiment that Americans shake on hamburgers and squirt on French fries by incalculable pints, quarts and gallons.

Catsup. Or ketchup, if you prefer.

Anyway, Sparky noted, wherever they are grown and processed now, chances are those tomatoes are harvested by mechanical pickers. Back in the local processing plant's boom times, though, they were harvested by migrant workers.

These migrant workers were also valued customers of Sparky's Doghouse.

Friday and Saturday nights in the middle of the harvests, Sparky recalled, the thirsts of folks who had spent hours laboring under the sun in those stifling, shimmering, endless fields picking tomatoes could have a real effect on business, and his stock.

"Sometimes we'd run out of beer," he recalled.

Beer could also tell you where the workers hailed from, he added, noting days when most of them had, say, traveled up from Texas.

"They'd always drink all the Schlitz first," Sparky said.

And if there seemed to be a run on Falstaff or Budweiser?

"They were from Florida," he explained.

At any given time when they were here, between 1,200 and 1,500 Mexican migrant workers would be living at the local camps in tiny, plain, sun-baked structures. On those thirsty nights, it wasn't uncommon for groups to pool their money to buy copious amounts of cold beer, which they would carry outside to drink in the cool air, the Doghouse hardly being able to handle groups of such size.

Still, they were welcome there.

"I loved them," Sparky said of those workers. "They were little trouble, unless the local hillbillies would get to aggravating them. Some of them we got to know like family. One guy, he was a crew leader, wore a Stetson hat and looked like Pancho Villa, came here in the fall for 46 years."

Besides the workers' peaceful nature, he added, the nature of their labor also added to mellow relations.

"You pick tomatoes all day," Sparky said, "the last thing you want to look for is a fight."

Nevertheless, he said, in 1973 there was a tragic incident involving the Doghouse and the workers that made the sort of unfortunate headlines that stick in folks' memories. Besides the Mexican workers, another operation had brought in Puerto Rican workers, and the two groups did not get along. One night, Sparky said, members of the latter group were accused of stealing change off the bar that belonged to the former group. A confrontation ensued, and soon both parties were heading out the door.

Outside, a young Mexican who thought he had been wronged pulled a gun and began firing at the Puerto Ricans, just as a Henry County sheriff's deputy transporting a prisoner was driving past.

Seeing the young man firing, the deputy braked to a stop, ordered him to drop the gun, and when he didn't, opened fire and killed him.

"Then all hell broke loose," recalled Sparky, who didn't own the Doghouse yet, but was a nighttime bartender there. "It turned kind of ugly."

Hundreds of Mexicans who thought the deputy had taken the Puerto Ricans' side rioted, forcing authorities to yank that cop off the streets for his own safety, plus impose martial law, which among other things also forced the shutdown of the Doghouse for four days.

It was a tense, scary time that made lots of headlines. Then, just like that, it was over.

That was the last of that sort of trouble at the Doghouse and Mt. Summit, Sparky said, adding that relations returned to normal and stayed that way, at least until the era of hand- picking tomatoes ended.

MENTOR AND PROTEGES

Run a successful tavern for as long as Sparky has, and you are going to learn a thing or two. Younger guys coming into the business, meanwhile, will want to pick your brain for the keys to longevity, satisfaction and making a decent living at it.

Two such guys are Jeff Viars and Bruce Horan.

Viars owns a place in New Castle called Scooter's Bar and Grill, and recalls being a youngster in Cadiz when he first saw Sparky.

"Best I can recollect, he was the big, tall guy walking around," he said, noting Sparky's reputation for athletics back then. "He was the big man around town. He was quite the thing to look up to."

When Viars bought Scooter's a dozen years ago, he sought out Sparky for saloonkeeper counseling.

"Sparky was quite instrumental in answering some of the questions I had when I bought it. It's a hard business, and he's helpful to anybody. The do's. The don'ts. Don't try this. You're foolish if you try that. I'll tell you one thing about Spark. He's a straight shooter. He'll tell you what he thinks. He's not going to intentionally steer you wrong."

Then Viars laughed.

"Of course, you can be a little bit of a straight shooter when you are his size."

What was an example of some advice he had adopted from Sparky?

"Don't frequent your own tavern," Viars said, then laughed again, suggesting he wasn't quite the stickler on that point that Sparky is.

"What he was saying was, don't lie around drunk in your own tavern all the time. You're a businessman first. Pleasure comes second."

Then he started speaking what you might call "Sparky-isms," familiar quotes to anyone who has been around Sparky long enough, such as "One more and we'll all go," and, "Well, that's how we'll do her then."

At this, Viars suddenly laughed again.

"I can imitate Sparky on the phone where you'd think you were talking to him," he said.

As for Horan, it was an Election Day when we walked inside his place shortly after noon, leaving the brilliant sunshine outside for The Ice House's far darker interior. It was an eye-catching place, with things like an old wheelchair hanging from the ceiling and a miniature version of the Butler University bulldog mascot, resting with lots of other memorabilia on a crowded shelf behind the bar. An authentic looking version of Joy's "I R NUTS" license plate caught your attention. There was your requisite "You look like I need another drink" sign, too, and some delicious-looking hamburgers frying on a grill. Meanwhile, an old black-and-white photograph of a stocky man in a headlock with what appeared to be a 25-pound lobster called up memories of when this place included a widely known fish buffet – "60 feet of succulent seafood" was its slogan – before a fire burned out the dining room back in 1978.

Obviously well used over time, the tavern portion of the place was 62 years old, making it more than twice as old as Horan, who is a mere 30.

It was six or seven years ago when Horan got to know Sparky after he and a buddy, who happened to be one of Joy's sons, flipped a house together and, with a certain amount of cash in hand, went looking for a place to invest it.

Buying an established bar like The Ice House? Sure, that was an option. Problem was, Horan kept asking owner Alex Burke – whose father, Harry, had been a mentor of Sparky's - if he wanted to sell it.

Sparky easily recalls those days, they being not that long ago. He also recalls telling Horan, "Every time you ask him about it, the price goes up." Still, Joy's son having long since moved on to other endeavors, when the old owner was ready to sell it, Horan was ready to buy it, and did so in 2012.

"He kind of adopted me as a father figure then," Sparky said.

These days, Sparky is still offering Horan advice, and the young saloonkeeper is still taking it.

Most of it, anyway.

"I listen to 99 percent of the things he tells me," Horan said, then laughed. "The other one percent, he's full of shit."

Then, between fetching beers for the seven or eight folks who were happily ensconced in his tavern, he continued on a more serious note.

"I've been fortunate enough to have Spark as a tutor," he said. "He'll offer advice whether I want to hear it or not. Spark's had 40 years of this. If I don't listen to him, I'm a true dumb ass."

As Horan worked, he wore a camouflaged baseball cap, camouflaged pants and a gray T-shirt shirt emblazoned with the letters NFS, sort of an official Ice House slogan which we shall leave un-translated, just on the outside chance this book is ever considered for stocking in a public library.

With that outfit and a couple days growth of beard, it seemed likely he was dressed far more casually than the majority of his classmates, scattered wherever they might be, from his graduating class at Butler University, where he earned a degree in exercise science.

Indeed, those two signed Butler basketballs so cherished by Sparky, came from Horan pulling strings. And the truth is, while their Butler playing days are a definite source of bonding between the two, Horan had the more notable career, a fact that was pointed out by one of his patrons this day – Steve Mason, owner of The Oasis tavern up in Muncie.

From a little sort of secondary bar in The Ice House where he had just finished lunch, Mason hollered, "He's still the leading three-point shooter in Butler history!"

If you know anything about the history of Butler University basketball, that's really saying something, the two teams that autographed those basketballs having made back-to-back appearances in the NCAA championship game in recent years. Naturally, the two team veterans enjoy watching Butler games together.

"No whiskey involved in watching those games, either," Horan lied.

So, just what sort of advice from Sparky has he incorporated in The Ice House? He pointed in the direction of the grill, where a visitor suddenly noticed a beautiful brown ham resting on a familiar-looking wire rack.

"That's some advice right there," he said.

And?

"The way to treat people. Be fair, be honest. I try to do that the best I can."

And?

"And a good honest smart-ass remark goes well, as long as you're genuine with it," at which point he yelled to a woman at the end of the bar. "Sorry! I couldn't see your Bloody Mary over there. It's kind of hidden in your cleavage."

What was his favorite thing about this business?

"The patrons," said Horan, who is a married man with a young daughter, plus a son on the way.

Then he added, "I've learned more in my two years and four months here than I did at my four years at Butler, that's for sure."

WOODWORKING SHOP

To get from Sparky's Doghouse to his woodworking shop you go south to New Castle, then west way into the country past Mount Lawn Speedway to the 93-acre farm he bought back in 1994. Of course, first he might take you east to the attractive home in a small, rural housing addition where he lives with Joy.

It's a nice, peaceful place that looks south over flat farm fields which come into view just beyond the many bird-feeding stations Joy maintains. It's a homey place, to be sure, with the sweet sort of signs you would never find in the Doghouse, like one that reads "Perch long, chirp much, sing often," and expertly done paintings of their vacation place on Lake Cumberland in Somerset, Ky., in fall and winter.

Perhaps the most notable thing about this place, though, is how much of the furniture in it Sparky has made.

A coffee table with a spring-loaded top narrows the distance between guests and their cups. There is a curio cabinet, a china cabinet and his grandmother's Hoosier kitchen cabinet, which he painstakingly restored. There's a computer desk, a trundle bed for his grandchildren, other assorted tables, a liquor cabinet and a gun cabinet in a room where a picture on the wall shows Sparky and the Piper Cherokee 180 he once owned, having acquired a private pilot's license and even an instrument flight rating. There's also the outhouse-shaped towel cabinet in the outhouse-themed bathroom, a quaint structure from which the toes of two work boots, plus a hint of lowered overalls, poke from a low gap in the door. Among other things, there is also an ornate bed frame.

"I tell everyone I was in a bordello down in New Orleans," he joked. "Near as I can tell, that's what the bed looked like."

By the way, the walnut he used to create it came from a tree that was blown down in a New Castle park one day.

"I got the pleasure of making it," he said, about that free wood. "It's better than buying it."

At any rate, take a look at all this furniture he has made, not to mention things like the church altar and pulpit pictured in one of his photo albums, and you come to understand that for Sparky, woodworking is less a hobby than a passion.

So it was that, having followed Sparky far out into the country, we eventually arrived at one of his two farms. At the time Sparky bought this one, it was owned by a fellow named Charlie Lockridge, a crusty old guy who didn't get along all that well with his neighbors, most of whom coveted his 93 acres themselves.

"All the neighbors wanted to buy it," Sparky said with a laugh, "so he sold it to me just to spite them."

His other farm is over near Cadiz, by the way, a place where he counts some of his most satisfying times being in the seat of his tractor, methodically mowing the tall grass growing along its boundary roadways.

"Oh, I love it," he said of the mowing.

Just not as much as he loves working in his shop.

Now, Sparky will be the first to tell you he loves a good drink on occasion, and when he bought his farms and equipped his woodworking shop, it was with that and the question of how to spend his retirement in mind.

"I've gotten to see several people drink themselves to death after retirement," he said, "and I didn't want to follow that."

As he spoke he was inside his shop, having crossed the small rectangle of sidewalk poured right outside the front entrance, one in which his name had been etched with a nail, along with the initials PBR which, despite what you might think, stands for Poured By Ralph.

Another name etched into the cement, though it was hard to make out, was John Rummel's.

Sparky's father, it should be noted, served in the Navy at sea during World War II as a carpenter's mate, but the mysterious effects of DNA aside, that's not really where he inherited his woodworking skills.

"I knew a little bit about woodworking," he said, "and I knew I enjoyed it."

But it was about the time when Rummel, a master woodworker, lost his job at a nearby shop, and Sparky came to the rescue, that his education really began..

"I said I'll build a woodworking shop, you can work in it and I'll play in it," Sparky said, crediting his friend with teaching him. "He was a real good teacher, because he never tried to do anything for you. Rummel was just an absolute perfectionist about his work. ... He taught me while he worked."

With dimensions of 32x48 feet, Sparky's shop is comfortably large and equipped with a dust-removal system he rigged up himself from four-inch PVC plumbing pipe. Upon walking in you pass under two things hung above the door, a horseshoe, about which there seems no particular story, and a one-foot segment of intricate crown molding, about which there is.

It goes as follows ...

After a while of being unemployed, Rummel returned to work, landing a job as a finish carpenter on the 20,000-square-foot home that was being built for legendary Indiana Pacers star Reggie Miller.

Totally taken with the project, Rummel arranged for Sparky to visit it, showing off amenities that included a 12-feet high, 12x14-feet clothes closet for Reggie, and a remotely controlled shoe rack that worked like a Lazy Susan for Mrs. Miller, one that would hold 300 pairs of shoes.

Still, it was that fancy molding that was most impressive, it costing $33 a foot.

"Reggie's got about a mile of it," Rummel told Sparky, and he meant that literally.

Elsewhere in the shop, neatly racked bar clamps, some up to 10-feet long, and wooden mallets big enough to knock out a buffalo, were hanging on a wall.

As for the power tools, there was a drill press, a band saw, a planer/joiner, a 37-inch dual drum sander, a router/shaper, a radial arm saw, a table saw, a morticing machine, a compound miter saw, a lathe and more. All told, Sparky said, he figured he spent $50,000 to $75,000 to equip his shop.

"He's pretty handy, I think, is what I hear," said Bruce Barefoot, himself a master carpenter and a Doghouse regular. "He's got a pretty nice shop. I'm sure it had a refrigerator in it, didn't it? That's the first tool you buy."

But if there was one, it wasn't obvious, and the fact that Sparky still has all his fingers made it seem certain that, if there was one, the only liquid stored inside it was Pepsi. Indeed, watching him trim a couple small pieces of wood was all the evidence one needed that liquor and table saws should never, ever mix.

Pushing the first piece of wood through the whirring, biting saw blade left one observer grimacing, picturing the obscene spray of blood, bone and gristle that would result as a sawn off thumb sailed through the air, pink and wet and trailing unmentionable stuff, looking for all the world like one of those ageless Red Hot Sausages that some bars sell from five-gallon jars of sharp, cloudy brine.

The neighbor who brought that wood in to be trimmed stepped through the doorway shortly after his Harley-Davidson was heard being downshifted on the nearby county road. When you own a shop like his, Sparky said, such visits were to be expected.

"You just can't imagine all the little jobs people will come up with," he noted, before setting off on what amounted to about three minutes work. "Every week somebody'll bring me a chair to fix."

Frankly, that seemed fine with him, though. If he didn't have a job that needed doing, he could step in here and quickly find *something* to occupy his hands, and mind.

"If I really wanted to," Sparky said, "I could spend 10 to 12 hours in here, and it'd feel like I'd been here 30 minutes."

As he spoke, he seemed sublimely content in a way that brought Joy's earlier words about Sparky and this place to mind.

"That's his safe place," she had said. "That's his sanctuary."

DOWN ON THE FARM

J.D. Masters and his son, Jason, are men of the land, and some of that land, among the whopping 5,000 acres they farm, is Sparky's.

"I've known him for 35 years, if not longer," said J.D., who often shows up at the Doghouse for Saturday breakfasts. "He's a good old boy."

That feeling is reciprocated by our favorite saloonkeeper, who takes great delight in mowing the miles of farmland – including his own - along the ditches that border the land. If he's not doing that, J.D. said, he might well be spraying weeds with the Gator.

"About the only thing Spark doesn't drive is the combine or the semis," he noted. "He takes it serious."

What's more, Sparky does all that for nothing but the joy of being outdoors and doing what he can to work the land.

Besides the help he gives them, though, the Masters also like Sparky for his entertainment value.

"He's an encyclopedia of jokes," J.D. said, with what almost sounded like amazement.

Then there's Sparky's penchant for trivia.

"He's one of a kind, that's for sure," Jason said, recalling times he has sat there shaking his head at something Sparky said. "You think, 'How in the hell did he come up with something like that? We ought to start writing this stuff down.' When did the (zeppelin) Hindenburg go down? He can tell you the date. He's one of a kind, that's for sure. He's done about everything."

Naturally, that would include baking hams, a meaningful endeavor to Jason, who counts himself a major fan of Sparky's ham sandwiches, and who celebrated his 21st birthday at the Doghouse.

Indeed, Jason's father used to have a waiting list of people wanting to buy his sausage, but he always made sure Sparky's orders were filled first.

But what else can you say of Sparky, about whom hundreds of tales are told?

For example, there was the tale of Sparky approaching the house of a well-known farm family in a bid to buy some cattle, only to be greeted by the farm wife wearing a mere cowboy hat and a gun belt.

"Some of the tales he tells," J.D. observed, "he's just unbelievable."

What especially came to Jason's mind, though, was the fact that Sparky scored the *last* basketball goal in the old Cadiz High School gym, and then the *first* basketball goal in the new Shenandoah High School gym.

Talk about the stuff of high school athletics legends ...

Come fall, he noted, when the work picks up on the farm, it can keep Sparky busy enough that he'll be late getting to one of his own favorite hangouts, the Eagles Club, for an evening's fun and relaxation. Even when it's not fall, J.D. added, the farm work doesn't hurt Sparky.

"It keeps him out of the Eagles until 4:30 or 5 o'clock," he said, with a quiet chuckle.

So what was his final take on Sparky?

"He's a good-hearted guy," J.D. said, recalling the time Sparky built him a desk, and also the time when he had open-heart surgery, and Sparky was one of the first guys who came to see him.

"He'll offer you anything," said the soft-spoken man you sense isn't given to effusive language under any circumstances. "It's just tough to beat him."

A BUDDY

Ask Jack Lee how long he has known Sparky and he answers, "We've been friends forever."

In terms of years, forever comes out to about 50.

Lee was just out of the Army back when he started running around Sulphur Springs with Sparky, who was younger but fit right into things. Eventually, they even lived together, with Lee moving into Sparky's place after he got a divorce.

As Lee noted with a laugh, "That was two or three girlfriends ago."

Over the years, they've had a lot of fun together.

"We've probably been to Las Vegas 10 times," he said, adding they have seen their share of NASCAR and Indy Car races, too. "We were just running around and drinking and having a good time. We had so many good times, and a lot of 'em you can't write down. We've had a wild good time."

That's not to say they didn't get some work done, too, though.

They actually did woodworking together as a business in Sparky's shop for 10 or 12 years, Lee noted.

"We started it as a hobby and it ended up being a job," he said. "We actually put all the insulation and all the flooring in it, too."

But back to leisure-time activities. The two have also played a lot of golf together, including one unforgettable round at a country club down in Ft. Meyers, Fla., back in 1986. There on the course, they watched as

70

a space shuttle was launched into the air, then seemed to take an odd course.

"You know Spark," Lee recalled. "He's always got an answer. He said it was the stages breaking away."

But when they got back to the club house, folks were gathered in shock around a television set. What they had witnessed, of course, was the explosion of the Space Shuttle Challenger, an unforgettable tragedy.

Less dramatic but also unforgettable, said Lee, a tall, balding man who sits quietly at the bar in the Doghouse, is something his friend Sparky once said to him.

"He said, 'You know, good friends can enjoy a moment of silence as much as they enjoy talking about something,'" Lee recalled. "I'll never forget that."

Sparky has been a joy in his life, Lee added.

"It's been a very good life, and he's been a very good friend," he said. "I'll tell you what, under all that rough appearance, he's got a heart as big as all outdoors. He's the most tenderhearted guy I've ever met."

DARRA

I've always found Sparky to be a joy to talk with on the phone, and that's a trait he shares with his daughter, Darra Moore. A resident of Seymour, she has the sort of warmth and spirit that immediately sets you at ease, along with a genuine, gentle laugh and an unassuming manner that makes you wish you were talking with her across a table instead of through phone lines. Mother of a son and a daughter, age 17 and 14, respectively, she is a stay-at-home Mom but sometimes works as a substitute teacher.

Apart from her conception, Sparky came into her life, or vice versa, about 13 years ago, when she was 30.

Sparky and Darra's mother weren't much more than kids when she became pregnant. They never married, and he made a conscious decision not to interfere in their lives, believing that would only complicate the situation for everybody.

"But I always knew I had a child," Sparky said.

Looking back on it now, Darra said her mother had some bitter feelings for how things had turned out, feelings she fully understands.

"She was a single mom," she explained. "It was rough on her."

Darra was a little girl of 2 in 1973 when her mother married, and she was adopted by the man who helped raise her.

"It takes somebody special to raise somebody's child like your own," Darra reflected, looking back on what she said was a happy childhood.

As for Sparky, he said his daughter was told he had walked away and didn't want anything to do with her.

But he knew where she went to school, and would avail himself of every opportunity to check out yearbooks and class pictures of the child he fathered, just to see how she was progressing. For her part, Darra somehow always felt a pull whenever she was driven past Sparky's Doghouse, though she had no idea why, and had declared more than once that someday, she would check out that mysterious place for herself.

It was in 2001 that Darra encountered a sister-in-law of Sparky's, who finally told her who her birth father was, and decided to seek him out.

"I just felt like it was time," said Darra, who noted she had begun wondering about her birth father as far back as seventh-grade. "I needed to find him. It just seemed like God needed me to find him. He needed to know that I forgave him."

Their first meeting came at a family birthday party, and things have been good between father and daughter from the very start, for which she is grateful.

"I could have met him and we would have hated each other," she said. "There was never any pressure (to bond or reconcile)."

Instead?

"He loves with all he has," she said of Sparky. "I never doubt that he loves me and my family. We're really blessed. My husband loves him. My kids love him. ... He's one of a kind. I've never met anyone like him. He's just larger than life. He's confident, intelligent."

An important part of their bonding came when she learned that for years, Sparky perused those aforementioned yearbooks and such, to keep tabs on how she was doing as best he could.

"For me to find out that he had his way of checking up on me, it really helped the relationship," Darra said. "He didn't really walk away. He did what he thought was best for me. He didn't forget about me. I think he had a lot of growing up to do."

These days, father, daughter and families all get together whenever possible, and truly enjoy each others' company. Indeed, Sparky and

Darra's adopted father know each other and are friends. Referring to the man in one brief conversation, Sparky gratefully and warmly called him "Saint Charlie," and for just an instant, his voice seemed to catch when he said it.

Among other nice things that have resulted from her relationship with her birth father, Darra said, is having a more complete picture of herself.

"I finally have all the pieces of my puzzle," she said, noting she now knows why, in a family full of early birds, she is usually late. So is Sparky. "And we're late for the same reasons. We don't want to sit there and wait. Now I know."

Beyond that?

"People say I look just like him. I act like him. We love to tell stories and jokes, and we love to make people laugh. I find that I stand like him. We have a lot in common."

Does she share Sparky's well documented sense of compassion?

"Well, I hope so," she said. "He just gives and gives. I just like spending time with him."

Looking back on their lives together now, the reality of those first 30 lost years doesn't weigh too heavily on her

"It doesn't really matter to me, I guess. I don't dwell on it. Whether he needed to grow up, whether I was better off without him, it all worked out for the best. ... There was a plan. There was a reason."

By the way, their relationship still takes some people by surprise.

"It's so funny when people find out he's my Dad," Darra said, laughing. "They say, 'What? I didn't know he was your father.' Hey, I didn't know either."

BACK IN THE DAY

*This story appeared as one of my Chow Hound pieces in the Dine
& Dish section of The Star Press so long ago, Sparky's Doghouse
was only The Cultural Center of Henry County at the time.*

Walk through the door of Sparky's Doghouse in Mt. Summit, and you're
not just entering another tavern.

"This is The Cultural Center of Henry County," professed longtime
owner Sparky Harris, who was behind the bar slicing ham in his estab-
lishment, a favorite of folks from far beyond the area, including Gov.
Mitch Daniels.

A handwritten note from Daniels, who has dined here four times,
commented on some appetizers and fresh bluegill filets he had enjoyed
in this laid-back place, where frosty beers chilled in a cooler while pool
balls quietly clacked.

Still, when most folks think of Sparky's, they think of ham.

"The signature sandwich here is ham," the owner contended.

Sure enough, a beautiful thick pink ham, its knobby bone protrud-
ing from its flat top like a handle, rested on a metal rack behind the bar,
one of 300 hams he prepares in a year. Of those, 100 are sliced up on
sandwiches for Sparky's customers. The other 200 are sold to folks at
Thanksgiving, Christmas, Easter and for dinner wakes after funerals,
some of them ordered directly by funeral homes.

"I always keep a ham in the rack," Harris said.

Tall, friendly and wearing the bright red suspenders from his buddy Phil Peterson's Albany tavern, Pete's Duck Inn, Harris said his career as a tavern owner was inevitable.

"That's the only thing I was ever qualified to do," joked the 62-year-old former REMC and Marhoefer Packing Co. employee, who began tending bar here in the early 1970s while he was playing basketball for Butler University.

He has owned Sparky's now for 38 years.

"I couldn't imagine doing anything else," he said of his work and his business, a down-home place where the only menu is a sign hung on the wall. Another sign reads, "If idiots grew on trees, this place would be an orchard."

Further adding to the décor are two basketballs signed by Butler's two recent NCAA national runner-up teams, and a mounted thee-pound, four-ounce bluegill about the size of a football, a state record fish.

"A buddy of mine caught that," Harris said, with an admiring glance over his shoulder.

The bluegill filets that a friend sometimes provides and our governor favors aren't listed on the menu. Nor are some of the other things that Harris whips up on certain days and gives away to hungry customers, like his chili, assorted casseroles or his summer salad, a combination of tomatoes, cucumbers and onions mixed with pasta and marinated in Italian dressing.

"It really is a favorite of all the farmers," Harris said.

Another thing you can buy that you won't find on the menu is Sparky's legendary pork-osaurus, a customer-designed, dinosaur-sized sandwich featuring a breaded tenderloin topped with sliced ham, one that even yours truly, the Chow Hound, feared he couldn't put a dent in. Ditto for the rest of the crew.

Instead, we stuck with the menu.

Chow Hound videographer Lathay Pegues ordered a steak sandwich and was rewarded with a huge one at $4.25. Chow Hound photographer Ashley Conti and I, meanwhile, went for the venerable ham sandwich at $3.25.

Frankly, I nearly swooned over mine, a pile of thinly sliced delicious ham, served with lettuce, mayo and hot cheese, a bit salty and redolent with that smoky flavor that in hams is sometimes labeled "country."

Was it the best ham sandwich I've ever eaten?

Well, I haven't exactly been keeping a running score of my life's ham sandwiches, but it was way, way up there, and my side of crisply deep-fried mushrooms at $2.25 was darned good, too. It's not surprising then that Bruce Horan, who was also sitting at the bar, said the ham sandwich was his favorite sandwich here, too.

Considerably younger than Harris, by the way, Horan is Butler University's all-time leading three-point shooter and now owns New Castle's The Ice House Tavern, work in which he gratefully acknowledged the mentoring of Sparky's owner, who is also his friend.

Other regulars here include teachers and executives who regularly drive or ride down from Muncie, but there are some other customers Harris especially aims to please, and not just the governor.

"In northern Henry County this is a good place for the working man," he said, discussing his modest prices and relaxed atmosphere and the skilled tradesmen who flock here to eat or quench their thirsts. "I've said for many years, you could get a house built here any afternoon."

CELEBRITIES

Can you believe that billionaire Donald Trump and late super-star Elizabeth Taylor were once regular customers of Sparky's Doghouse?

No?

Good, because they weren't, of course, and you'd have to be a moron to think they ever were. But do you want to know *why* they weren't? It's because neither one of them was cool enough to be customers of The Cultural Center of the Universe, that's why. Well, yeah, OK, OK. Elizabeth Taylor was plenty cool enough. I mean, hey, we're talking about Liz here, for cryin' out loud. But Trump? Not even close. Not even with a better haircut, which, frankly, would be the only kind of haircut he could possibly get.

But lesser celebrities have found their way through the door.

As we mentioned earlier, Indiana's former governor, Mitch Daniels, was here four or five times, and even dined on Sparky's hog nuts, which to our way of thinking made him a guy the voters could put their trust in.

We mentioned this earlier, too, but professional wrestler Dick the Bruiser also used to come in for a beer and a sandwich after matches in New Castle. In fact, he wandered in the very first night that Sparky ever worked the bar as a kid, way before he bought the place.

Another celebrity? We've mentioned Whitey Shively, too, the auctioneer who ended up playing the team doctor in the classic Indiana basketball movie "Hoosiers."

Others?

A lot of race car drivers have made a proverbial pit stop here, like four-time Indianapolis 500 winner Al Unser and three-time winner Johnny Rutherford.

"This was right on their way to Winchester Speedway," Sparky explained.

That's still a great track, of course, but back in the day before big-time racing went so corporate, it regularly drew some of the hottest "shoes" in the country to compete in sprint cars.

"Nobody'd bug them," Sparky said of the racing stars and his clientele. "That's one of the reasons they stopped here. But everybody knew who they were."

So that's pretty cool. Still, when we're talking about celebrities, we can't neglect to mention New Castle's Jamie Ferrell.

Who, you ask, is that?

Back in 1997, the comely young lass was a Playboy Playmate, a centerfold no less, and dated Doghouse customer Kevin "Beaver" Barnett.

Sparky noted he had at least one interesting exchange with her, saying he knew her grandfather, plus revealing the interesting fact that her grandfather's old girlfriend and his old girlfriend shared the same Social Security number.

How, she wondered, could that be?

They were the same woman, Sparky told her.

By the way, he added of Ferrell, "She's still a real good looking gal."

BUSTED

Sparky will be the first to tell you he's had a wonderful experience owning the Doghouse, but there is one incident that still sticks in his proverbial craw.

It was about five years ago when a female state excise cop walked in, marched behind the bar like she owned the place and took the money from the cash register holding the Indiana gambling proceeds, a rather brazen act which set the saloonkeeper's teeth on edge. Not long afterward, she did it again, and in a similarly haughty manner that didn't endear her to anyone, Sparky least of all.

"She just went back there and emptied the cash register is what she done," Sparky recalled, adding that this time, he went behind the bar with her and clapped her lightly on the shoulder.

This, as things turned out, was not a good move. Erupting in anger, her reaction had the unfortunate effect of launching Sparky's customers along the bar into fits of laughter, which only angered the cop more. Taking Sparky severely to task, she cited him and threatened him with further action, a threat which soon proved not to be an empty one. Indeed, it was a short time later that, having left the Doghouse, he was told by an employee to come back to the bar as soon as possible.

"When I walked in the back door," he remembered, "you could have heard a mouse piss on a cotton ball."

Turns out he was being charged with assaulting a police officer, something that still rankles him no end.

"That was the most underhanded thing I ever had done to me," Sparky recalled, having just delivered beers to a couple thirsty guys at a table in his place. "I told them, if there's a law against being a smart ass, I'm guilty. But I've touched my mother a lot harder than I touched her."

Nevertheless, Sparky soon found himself cuffed and hauled off to the hoosegow, where he spent the next 12 hours sitting with the other miscreants before bonding out of jail for $5,000. Putting his lawyer on the case cost him another $10,000, but before long he heard from the county prosecutor, excise prosecutor and county sheriff that they believed he had been the victim of a miscarriage of justice, and expressing their apologies.

In the end, the whole incident went away after he paid a $100 fine and wrote the cop a letter of apology.

"And I misspelled apologize on purpose," Sparky added, laughing.

ODES TO SPARKY'S DOGHOUSE (AND RELATED SUBJECTS)

A LIMERICK

Some guys like girls who act like sluts,
And some dig girls with shapely butts,
But as for old Sparky,
He shuns such malarkey,
Just give him a handful of Nuts

HAIKU

ham in a metal
rack, sliced and on its way to
my empty belly

FREE VERSE

Pride of Mt. Summit, wrapped in white,
like a beautiful cloud that floats over the town, but instead
of raining rainwater, rains Budweiser,
and sometimes sends hail, too, but not like
the icy kind of hail that can hurt
when it hits you on the forehead, but the
soft kind that doesn't hurt at all,
because
it's actually deep-fried mushrooms.

And Sparky stands behind the bar, resplendent in neon-colored
suspenders, holding up his pants, like the
Doghouse supports the spirits
of all who take solace, and maybe even a snort or two of whiskey, there.

VERSE THAT RHYMES

You leave the four lanes, then turn to the west
To get to the place, that you love best.
No it's not a McDonald's or Pizza King
But a cool little place where the customers bring
Their cares and their worries, and leave them behind,
And anything else that weighs on their mind.

They may drink some beer, the best drink invented,
Which they say's never purchased, but only rented,
Or maybe some bourbon, some vodka or gin
But never so much that to drink more's a sin.
For the folks at the Doghouse all know that it
Is never a good thing, to drink 'til you're shit-

Faced drunk, it's not wise, it's a hassle, it's rude
And can lead to behavior that's undoubtedly crude
To which the good owner, would be much averse,
In this, The Cultural Center of the Universe.
For Sparky, above all, is a gentlemanly gent
With a peaceful, well-mannered, angelic bent,

From his head past his collar, to the cuffs of his pants,
Plus he stands six-foot-seven, so why take a chance
On pissing him off, and then being barred,
From this place where even Mitch Daniels has starred
While our governor, walking our state's hallowed halls
As a customer munching some tasty hog balls?

And some bluegill filets and some other fine stuff
No, to be barred from here, would be very rough.
See, your status among the fine folks of Mt. Summit
Would go down the tubes, would tumble, would plummet
And you would be seen as the worst sort of boozer
In short you'd be seen as the worst sort of loser.

See, the folks who are in here between Sparky's walls
From the north-facing entrance, to its southerly stalls
Are God's gift to bartenders, a wonderful crowd
The kind of folks who make you so proud
To say you belong here in this special place
That never fails to bring, a smile to your face.

A COLUMN

(I've been writing a personal column, first for the old Muncie Evening Press and then for The Star Press, for more years than I like to remember. If I were writing one now about Sparky's Doghouse and Sparky, it would probably read something like this.)

If you had asked me, even as recently as six months ago, if the day would come when I would write a book about Sparky Harris and Sparky's Doghouse, I would have looked at you askance. It's not that I didn't like him, because I do, and it's not because I didn't like the Doghouse, because I like it, too.

I guess it's just the fact that putting that sort of effort into a book that probably won't sell to anyone but Sparky's family, my family (at least, I *hope* my wife will buy a copy) and a few diehard fans of the Doghouse, didn't seem to make a lot of sense from a financial perspective.

But then, I came to my senses.

It was a gray winter's Saturday, and my wife Nan and I had just downed a couple ham sandwiches for lunch, while I had downed a couple other things, too, a meal at which Sparky had visited our table to offer what might best be called Sparky-isms. They, and those couple other things, had kept me cracked up and feeling warm, fuzzy feelings for this comfortable little dive. Now, on the drive home, with Nan behind the wheel and me in the passenger seat, it hit me.

"Man," I said, "he's got a book there."

I mean, for one thing, Sparky oozed character. It was obvious in his jokes, his wisecracks, his stories and his general air.

The Doghouse itself oozed character, too. Lord knows I had been in some noteworthy bars before, but this totally unpretentious place had it in spades, from the Information Center in the corner to the undeniably funky restrooms to the huge honking hunk of ham on the counter alongside the grill.

And I knew for a fact that the customers in this joint, *being* characters, oozed character, too. It was definitely a small-town, rural, working-man's place. That was obvious from the faded overalls, worn work boots, green John Deere caps and heavily-whiskered chins of the folks who had sidled up to the bar, even the women.

Ha-ha! I am just kidding about that last part. Doghouse women are some of the sweetest, most feminine and beautiful representatives of their gender you will find anywhere.

But yeah, this was a working-class joint.

And yet, I knew it was also a favorite hangout of those effete snobs from that metropolis up Muncie way, from which all sorts of weekday suit-wearers journeyed every weekend for down-home doses of the stuff that makes life worth living.

At any rate, suddenly the idea of writing a book about the place took hold of me and wouldn't let go. I could barely wait until the following week when Nan and I could get back down for lunch again and I could ask Sparky, "How would you feel about me writing a book about your place?"

He gave it about two seconds thought and said, "Sure."

Anyway, that's how this whole enterprise started, and since jotting that first note in my purple notebook, I've only gotten more enthused about it.

To tell you the truth, at this point I don't care if the book sells only 20 copies, though if that figure turned out to be more like 20,000, that would be fine with me, too. What I really like thinking about is, at least I've put the story of a special guy and a special place at a special time down on paper.

I also like thinking that, maybe far, far, far into the future, some New Castle kid with a big round head, antennas poking from his ears and flashing yellow eyes - some youngster whose Mom has transported him through time to the Henry County Library in 2014 on the proverbial "way back" machine, while she gets her feelers manicured, a kid who has been raised on protein injections for the first tenth of his projected 150 year lifespan - will insert a copy of "Tails From Sparky's Doghouse" in his brain's auto-info-slot, read a few paragraphs and sigh, thinking, "Man, I wish I could have had a beer and a ham sandwich there."

SPARKY'S MENTOR

Ask Sparky whose advice and counsel he most cherished, and continues to cherish, as owner of The Doghouse, and he'll tell you Salem Shively, though it wasn't in matters of business fashion.

"To look at him, you'd think he didn't have a dime," Sparky said, warmly recalling the man who had such an impact on his life. "He'd wear two different shoes, two different socks ... But I learned so much from him. He was the smartest man I ever knew.

Indeed, Salem was smart, and unique. The co-owner, with John Rutherford, of a bowling alley in New Castle, he had graduated from high school at age 13, and became a journalism major at Indiana University before leaving there at 16.

Another point of interest?

"He was one of the most accomplished bridge players in the world," Sparky continued, noting that Salem won a Life Master award in 1967, and cultivated quite a following with his writing about the game, which if you've never followed it in print, is like reading Sanskrit. "Every now and then a stranger would walk in with a piece of paper in their hands and ask what card should he lead with? When should you try to finesse? It might be anything."

Beginning in 1960 Salem also indulged another passion of his, one for the Olympics, attending the games in Rome and continuing to do so through those in Los Angeles, shortly before his death from leukemia in 1984.

Perhaps with his early years as a journalism major in mind, Sparky added, he would send articles about the Games back home for publication in New Castle's newspaper The Courier Times.

The most amazing thing about Shively, though, is to picture him sitting inside the Doghouse of a morning, reading The Wall Street Journal, about as incongruous a sight here as would be watching a goat amble up to the bar to order a beer.

The world traveler came in for breakfast about 8:30 every morning, and he never turned away a question from Sparky, who was just 24 when their mentor-protégé relationship began.

In a way, Sparky hinted, their rendezvous smacked of karma.

"I knew *nothing* of how to run a business," he said, explaining he took to asking his older friend an important question every day. "Oddly enough, there in front of me every morning was probably the greatest wealth of information I'd ever seen. He'd give you the answer, or if he didn't know it, he'd say 'I'll tell you tomorrow' and go to the library and get a book."

Sparky recalled that one day, back about the time of Jimmy Carter's election as president, he offhandedly asked Salem, "What number president is he?' He said 'Gimme a piece of paper and a pen and I'll tell you.' He'd write a little. Drink a little coffee. After a while he handed me that paper. Thirty-ninth. He'd written down every president spelled correctly, and the year they were elected to office and the year they left office or died. And he done that while he was reading the newspaper."

His young friend was, to say the least, suitably impressed.

"He's the only man I ever knew in my life that I think was smart enough to be president," Sparky said.

Still, he continued, most of his questions weren't related to political history.

The first advice Salem ever gave him, Sparky said, is still the best.

"Let those other guys be president or vice-president and give all their speeches. You be secretary of the Treasury. That way, you're the first to count the money."

That advice has stayed with him.

"I've never forgotten that," Sparky said, "and whenever I have a decision to make, I refer back to what Salem would have done, and I do that to this very day. He was totally honest. He never lied to himself, or anybody else. He was a very special friend."

SPARKY REPRISED

We were at a table on a typical Saturday at lunch. Lots of folks were nursing beers, and more than a few were dining on sandwiches. My dad and I ordered a couple grilled tenderloins, then scooped ourselves a couple bowls of Sparky's summer pasta salad when he carried it around. He made sure that everybody who wanted some had some, then joined us at our table.

Something in the way we asked about things put him in a reflective mood.

"I've been here through the real good times, and I was here when they went flat," he said. "But my customers were true. This little tavern is kind of recession-proof. It's been here since they repealed Prohibition.

"I've always said, whenever I quit, I'm gonna take out a full-page ad and say thanks to all the people who ever came in here and spent their money."

Because he sounded so reflective, I mentioned a talk I'd had not long before with his protégé Bruce Horan, owner of The Ice House tavern, asking if he could ever imagine the Doghouse without Sparky?

Turned out, he thought about it, and couldn't.

"It wouldn't be the same," he said.

Now I asked Sparky the same thing, and he answered exactly as Horan had.

"It wouldn't be the same," he said, wrapping up in five words the reason why that thought just didn't compute. Life is change, smart people argue, but sometimes, somewhere, for sanity's sake, some things need to stay the way they were.

Surrounded by the four walls of this old saloon, Sparky mentioned how there had once been a time when he considered tearing them down and building a more modern place.

"But it finally dawned on me one day, that was part of what made this place special," he said. "There are lots and lots of people that will remember the things that have happened in here. I'm sure they'll be proud to say they visited this place."

Then, for just a moment, he got quiet again and looked around.

"God," Sparky finally said. "If these old walls could talk..."

LAST CALL

It was 11 p.m. on a Tuesday night, and Karen Drumm, better known in these parts as Cheeseburger, was an hour away from finishing her shift. Every stool along the bar was occupied, while a couple young fellows – Eric Corn and John Evans – were getting in a last few games of pool.

Eric was making short work of the Bloody Marys he kept buying from Karen, substantial drinks made with generous pours of vodka, dabs of horseradish, numerous shakes of Frank's hot sauce and plenty of chubby green olives, all generously topped with lots of salt and pepper. They seemed more like meals than drinks.

"Bruce Corn is a legend in here," he said proudly of his father, sipping Bloody Mary through a straw and sounding like he was feeling no pain. "Yep, I'm carrying on the old family tradition."

Earlier, Scott Rowe had been draining a beer at the bar.

"I come down here once a month or so," he casually mentioned with an innocent look, as the women around him, including Vickie Chalfant, erupted with laughter.

"He's what you call a regular," she explained with a beautiful smile, casting an admiring glance at Rowe, who then owned up to the fact that he was in here more often – you might even say a *lot* more often – than once a month.

Meanwhile, as the minutes of this day ticked away, the Doghouse gradually began to empty. By now the bar was gleaming under the lights as Karen wiped it down. On the television, the suited image of a weather forecaster, the screen behind him full of green, yellow and red radar hits, lost his bid for attention to the country tune that was playing. Then David Letterman appeared, but nobody paid any attention to him, either.

Two strangers who had been sitting at the end of the bar headed for the door and Karen told them, "Be careful, darlin'."

By now, Allison Bainbridge, wearing a sleeveless white T-shirt and a Harley-Davidson baseball cap, was pushing and arranging the barstools against the bar with military precision.

"I pretty much live here,'" she admitted with a smile, noting her home was just across the street.

Then with the sudden clack of a lone pool ball entering a pocket, Karen said, "Perfect timing, guys," and the last folks inside headed for the door.

Just like that, the Doghouse went quiet.

The clock read midnight.

Another day had ended at The Cultural Center of the Universe.

John W. Carlson is a features writer in Muncie, Ind., for The Star Press, where his columns, which have also been published by the newspaper in the collections "Individually" Wrapped" and "Nice Try," have won a Best of Gannett Award. His work was cited in Ray Banta's book "More of Indiana's Laughmakers," and his humorous crime stories have appeared in Red Herring, Ellery Queen and Alfred Hitchcock mystery magazines.

Cover photos by Jordan Kartholl

"Over a decade on the road, I got to know almost every little diner and dive in the state of Indiana, and I can testify that Sparky's ranks with my very top favorites."

Former Indiana Gov. Mitch Daniels

Made in the USA
Charleston, SC
02 November 2014